BANTAMS OVE

BANTAMS OVER WEMBLEY

Bradford City's
Miracle Season

Dave Fletcher

Scratching Shed Publishing Ltd

First published by Scratching Shed Publishing Ltd in 2013
Registered in England & Wales No. 6588772.
Registered office:
47 Street Lane, Leeds, West Yorkshire. LS8 1AP
www.scratchingshedpublishing.co.uk
ISBN 978-0957559356

A catalogue record for this book is available from the British Library.

Typeset in Warnock Pro Semi Bold and Palatino
Printed and bound in the United Kingdom by
Charlesworth Press, Flanshaw Way, Flanshaw Lane,
Wakefield, WF2 9LP

"Wem-ber-lee, Wem-ber-lee...
We're the famous Bradford City
and we're going to Wem-ber-lee..."

(repeat)

The Author

Dave Fletcher reported on Halifax Town from Conference to Football League and down to the Unibond League for thirteen years. He thought he had seen everything until, in 2012, he was given the opportunity to cover Bradford City for BBC Leeds.

Dave began his career writing about Goole Town, so it could only get better. He advanced, via stints covering rugby league clubs Castleford and Featherstone Rovers, to the Press Association and then Halifax.

It was a route that taught him to expect little and savour the big moments, a life lesson he has never forgotten.

Acknowledgements

I have to thank my expert summarisers - John Hendrie, Wayne Jacobs, Graham Mitchell, Mike Harrison and, on a couple of occasions, Darren Moore - for making my job so easy throughout the campaign.

Thanks also go to City press officer Mark Harrison for his help in my first season covering the club, and the players and coaching staff for putting up with the questions week after week.

Without BBC Radio Leeds sports editor Gareth Jones, who offered me the chance to cover City, none of this would have been possible.

And it is a real team effort at the station, so further thanks to Katherine Hannah, Adam Pope, Nick Hatton and Paul Ogden in front of the mic, and the techies Loz Whitaker, Ronan Sully and Leanne Chuter, without whom I would never have made it to air.

I am also grateful to Gary Chadwick and Gintare Karpaviciute for their photographic input.

Contents

npower
BC
AFC

Foreword

By Gary Jones

I had been at Rochdale for a long time, but the last year I was there we were relegated and me and the manager didn't really see eye to eye.

I had another year left on my contract, but heard that Bradford City were interested. When I met Phil Parkinson we spoke at length about how the club was a sleeping giant and how, if we could get a winning mentality and a winning team, the place could take off.

That really swung my decision to come.

I knew there were good players here already and, with the addition of others, I thought we were really strong and had a good chance.

After the slump of the previous couple of years we felt we could really achieve something.

Without a doubt the expectations were high, but I don't think anyone could have foreseen what eventually happened.

Inspirational figure: Bradford City skipper Gary Jones and friend Gintare Karpaviciute

Wembley finals and getting promoted is ridiculous, but miracles do happen in football and I think getting to the Capital One Cup final was just that.

We re-grouped after that game and to lose just two out of the next fifteen was an absolutely phenomenal achievement.

It was amazing how we did it.

We were ten or 12 points away from the play-offs and a lot of people had written us off . They thought we would finish in mid-table.

But we knew what could be achieved if we could get a good run together; momentum is massive in football and that carried us right through.

A lot of teams had been in the play-off places all season and that can be quite difficult.

But we came from nowhere, sealing our place in the top seven in the second-to-last game of the season.

We sneaked in the back door.

Objective: Promotion

"On such things do
success and failure hinge..."

Successive seasons finishing 18th in League Two was simply not good enough for a team like Bradford City.

The fans made that clear, although they still snapped up season tickets in the kind of numbers most fourth-tier teams can only dream of attracting.

As a result, manager Phil Parkinson, still to celebrate his first anniversary in the job, was given just one objective: promotion.

His route as far as the squad was concerned was quality rather than quantity. But there were still 11 permanent signings made in the close season.

Andrew Davies and Will Atkinson were snapped up, having completed loan spells during the previous campaign, and former loanee Nathan Doyle returned to the club.

City fought off strong competition to bring in veteran midfielder Gary Jones from Rochdale and Garry Thompson from Scunthorpe. And Alan Connell, a striker who played a major part in Swindon's promotion three months earlier, also arrived along with Northern Ireland international Rory McArdle.

There was a sprinkling of youth with Zavon Hines signing from Burnley, Carl McHugh joining from Reading's squad, Stephen Darby from Liverpool and James Meredith, a double Wembley winner in May, arriving from York.

Old favourites remained; Nahki Wells would sign an extension to his contract while James Hanson and Matt Duke would steal the headlines in January.

Jon McLaughlin, Luke Oliver and Kyel Reid were also retained, although the latter pair would have their participation restricted by serious injuries.

Yet anyone who watched Parkinson's new-look side against League One Bury, in the Bantams' one and only home warm-up game seven days prior to a trip down the M1 to Nottingham for the first round of the Capital One Cup, would have been less than optimistic about their chances of defeating County.

City had been a distant second best, going down 3-0 to the Shakers on Saturday 4 August, and the manager had looked a little 'upset' in the immediate aftermath.

But the fans - as they did throughout the season wherever the team was playing - travelled in numbers to Meadow Lane. And they were rewarded handsomely with Hanson's extra-time half-volley, which settled the tie in favour of a Bradford team boasting six summer signings.

It could have been very different had Yoann Arquin not managed to hit the bar from a couple of yards out inside the 90 minutes.

On such things do success and failure hinge.

Meadow Lane, like so many grounds, was almost

entirely rebuilt in the 1990s, but is still overshadowed by its near neighbour the City Ground home of Forest.

But County are, quite correctly, very proud of being the oldest league club in existence and were expected to challenge in League One under Keith Curle.

It was a strange game in many ways, with more than a feel of a glorified pre-season friendly than the opening encounter of a competition that would eventually propel the club, its players and the whole city into the national limelight.

In keeping with that feeling, City's reward for their upset victory was far from mouth-watering - a trip to Championship side Watford, recently bought by a wealthy Italian family and clearly geared up for a tilt at the top flight.

For the Bantams, there was still little to suggest it was going to be an historic season.

League Cup - First Round
August 11 - Notts County (A) W 1-0 (*after extra-time*)
City scorer: Hanson, 95
Duke, Darby, Meredith, Oliver, McArdle, Reid (Doyle 104), Thompson (Baker 74), Atkinson, Jones, Hanson, Connell (Wells 61). Unused substitutes: McLaughlin, Brown, Bass, Hannah
Referee: Deadman
Attendance: 3,460

Flying the flag: City fans began the season in the hope of big things *Gintare Karpaviciute*

The Campaign Commences

"Five first-half goals did the trick, they usually do..."

Before tackling the Hornets at the end of August, City had to start their League Two campaign and initially that meant a trip to the deep south - Gillingham.

Closer to Paris than Bradford, in terms of distance if not café culture, Kent was in the grip of a heatwave with temperatures rising rapidly on the drive down.

And there was a funfair in full flow on what passes for the seafront; in reality it is a small patch of sand on the banks of the Medway Estuary.

It was not quite so warm in West Yorkshire when the fans set off at 8am, so by the time they were stuck in traffic on the M25, at least one of the fleeces were a little redundant.

Despite playing reasonably well, a 3-1 defeat did little to help the travelling supporters 'housed' in the open end at the Priestfield Stadium, turning pinker by the minute under the blistering sun.

In fairness, the Gills were gifted their second goal after a rash challenge in the area by Will Atkinson, one of the players who would be pivotal to the team's success over the season. And there was some consolation for City, with Nahki Wells opening his account for the campaign, also from the penalty spot.

It is a long way back to Bradford from Kent when you have nothing to show for your efforts. And it would be a while before the bright red faces of the sunburned City fans calmed down.

Fortunately, they only had three days to wait for their favourites' first league victory of the season.

Micky Mellon-mentored cash-rich Football League newcomers Fleetwood were first up at Valley Parade on Tuesday 21 August. And a generally uneventful evening was brightened on the hour, when Hanson headed his debut League Two goal of the campaign to secure the three points.

The saddest part of the night was that, in their side's first-ever season of League football, just 182 away fans made the relatively short trip across the Pennines.

They were, after all, unlikely to play in such impressive surroundings again over the course of the season.

The first week of league action finally exploded into life the following weekend, when AFC Wimbledon arrived in West Yorkshire and were soundly thrashed.

Five first half goals did the trick - they usually do.

The pick of them was not a 30-yard screamer - or a neat finish following a silky passing move.

It was a comedy own goal from hapless on-loan defender Curtis Haynes-Brown, whose miserable day ended with a trip to hospital when he was forced to leave the field on a stretcher after a second-half neck injury.

Happily, he suffered no lasting damage and, in the

space of the opening eight days, City were able to reflect on being handily placed in the table.

By the time Haynes-Brown sliced the ball into his own net, Wells had already opened the scoring for the hosts. A long-range Andrew Davies free kick made it 3-0 before a Byron Harrison header finally got the Dons on the scoreboard. Rory McArdle and Hanson finished the job.

In contrast, the early rounds of the Capital One - aka League Cup - rarely set the pulses racing and the wide open stands of Vicarage Road, used to Championship fare, were never going to be full for the visit of League Two City.

The first triumph of the game came when a BBC pass proved sufficient to avoid having to pay a barely believable £12 to leave the car in the car park closest to the ground.

Given the tough late August schedule - five games in 17 days - six changes to the starting line-up suggested it could be a long night.

Watford, as one would expect under Gianfranco Zola, passed the ball to within an inch of its life.

There was no way through on the left so, with all the precision of a team of engineers, the home side switched play to the right.

Play moved from side to side all night and when winger Ikechi Anya broke the deadlock in the 71st minute with a 25-yard shot, claret and amber hearts sank.

From the scaffolding commentary position in front of the condemned Vicarage Road stand it looked all over for the Bantams. But Kyel Reid levelled from the left and Garry Thompson bagged a dramatic last-gasp winner from close range to send City through to round three, both goals coming from set-plays.

Thompson, who would have to work hard to establish himself as a regular in the side, received the thanks of all those who saw him post-match. Not specifically for his goal, it meant there would be no extra-time and we could get back in our handily parked cars and return north.

A second 'giant-killing' act of the season already had failed to cause much of a stir in footballing circles; there was scarcely a mention of it on national radio as the fans slalomed their way through the roadworks on the way home.

It did mean another game, of course. And when City were paired at home with fellow League Two outfit Burton Albion, the possibility of a decent draw in round four was vaguely exciting.

Less exciting, from a Bradford perspective at least, was the first Yorkshire derby of the season at Rotherham.

League Two
August 18 - Gillingham (A) L 1-3
City scorer: Wells 62 (pen)
Duke, Darby (Davies 83), McArdle, Oliver, Meredith, Thompson (Hines 58), Reid, Atkinson, Jones, Hanson, Connell (Wells 57). Unused substitutes: Doyle, McLaughlin, Hannah, McHugh
Referee: Russell. Attendance: 5,127

League Two
August 21 - Fleetwood Town (H) W 1-0
City scorer: Hanson 59
Duke, McArdle, Oliver, Meredith, Davies, Reid, Jones, Doyle (Atkinson 77), Hines (Thompson 65), Wells (Darby 87), Hanson. Unused substitutes: Connell, Hannah, McHugh, McLaughlin
Referee: Duncan. Attendance: 9,224

League Two

August 25 – AFC Wimbledon (H) W 5-1

City scorers: Wells 3; Haynes-Brown 13 (og); Davies 31; McArdle 37; Hanson 45

Duke, Meredith, Davies, Oliver, McArdle, Jones, Doyle (Thompson 74), Reid, Hines (Atkinson 74), Hanson, Wells (Connell 79). Unused substitutes: McLaughlin, Darby, McHugh, Hannah

Ref: Miller. Attendance: 9,536

League Cup - Second Round

August 28 – Watford (A) W 2-1

City scorers: Reid 84; Thompson 90

McLaughlin, Darby, Meredith (Hanson 76), Oliver, McHugh, McArdle, Thompson, Atkinson, Jones (Doyle 61), Connell, Hines (Reid 59). Unused substitutes: Duke, Bass, Hannah, Baker

Referee: Sarginson. Attendance: 5,560

League Two				31 August 2012
		P	*GD*	*Pts*
1	Oxford Utd	3	5	9
2	Gillingham	3	4	9
3	Cheltenham	3	3	7
4	**Bradford**	3	3	6
5	Port Vale	3	3	6
6	Exeter	3	1	6
7	Accrington	3	0	6
8	Torquay	3	2	5
9	Northampton	3	1	5
10	Rotherham	3	2	4
11	Morecambe	3	1	4
12	York	3	0	4
13	Fleetwood	3	0	4
14	Wycombe	2	1	3
15	Burton Albion	3	0	3
16	Aldershot	3	0	3
17	Wimbledon	3	-7	3
18	Chesterfield	3	-1	2
19	Rochdale	3	-2	2
20	Bristol Rovers	2	-2	1
21	Southend	3	-3	1
22	Dag & Red	3	-3	1
23	Plymouth	3	-3	1
24	Barnet	3	-5	1

September Song

"Even the presence of pies - and hot pies at that - could not temper the disappointment..."

The Millers' magnificent New York Stadium is a triumph of design, combining the best of the new with more than a splash of character so often missing from the flat-packed venues that have sprouted over the last 15 years or so.

The ground was just about sold out on Saturday 1 September, but the 2,267 who made the short journey south from Bradford never really recovered from the concession of a first-minute goal.

It was actually just 55 seconds in when Michael O'Connor opened the scoring, this commentator being only halfway through reading out the teams for BBC Leeds listeners as the ball hit the back of the net.

And two goals from City old boy Gareth Evans, whose over zealous celebration of his first incensed the travelling fans, did nothing to improve their humour.

Rotherham went on to complete a comfortable 4-0

win and even the presence of pies - and hot pies at that - in the Press room could not temper the disappointment.

At that early stage of the campaign, though, it was a matter of onwards and upwards - sort of.

The contrast between New York and old Accrington, in terms of facilities, could hardly be starker.

In South Yorkshire you watch the action unfold from up in the gods; in East Lancashire you get the feeling you are actually on the playing surface.

And you can forget any notion of leg-stretching for the duration of the match.

That is no criticism of one of the smallest clubs playing in the League, just a statement of fact. And the overall experience at the Crown ground is no poorer for it.

It took a late equaliser from Alan Connell to salvage a point from the trip, after the hosts went ahead when Padraig Amond tapped home against the run of play on 73 minutes. Ten minutes later, Hanson flicked the ball on to the substitute, Connell, who fired home from distance to notch his first score for the club. But City were in 14th place and, although the season was young, underachieving.

It was with some relief, then, that a hat-trick of wins, at home to Barnet and Morecambe and away at Oxford, lifted Phil Parkinson's men back into the top four.

It seemed a shame for the 70 travelling fans in the away section of Valley Parade that the sum total of Barnet's ambition was to get a goalless draw.

Their not-so cunning plan worked until half-time as City struggled to break them down.

But patience on and off the pitch was the key, something that would stand the City faithful and players in good stead over the course of the campaign, and the home support was rewarded with three goals in ten second-half minutes. First, Hanson headed in a deflected Gary Jones free-kick. Then, when Bees keeper Graham Stack lost a Kyel Reid cross, Connell slotted the ball home before Andrew Davies completed the 3-0 rout with a header from another Jones free-kick inside the six-yard box.

City were up to seventh. Barnet rock bottom.

On Tuesday 18 September, Morecambe arrived in West Yorkshire unbeaten on their travels, but again it was City who emerged victorious, 3-1. And for the fourth game in a row on home soil, which meant they had made their best start to a league campaign at Valley Parade for 55 years.

When City set that record, the Shrimps were plying their trade in the Lancashire Combination.

Something was clearly stirring, although the game itself was nothing more than routine for Parkinson's side with the highlight a fifth goal of the season for Hanson, a minute before the break. Second-half scores from Reid and Jones either side of a Jack Redshaw goal for the visitors did the rest.

Having watched Oxford-boss Chris Wilder's Halifax Town side for five seasons in a previous existence behind the microphone, it would have been nice to have had a chat at the Kassam Stadium.

But in the midst of a poor run of results - a 2-0 home defeat to City was one of seven successive reverses - the Sheffield-born boss was only just speaking to the local boys by the time the media vacated the ground 80 minutes after the final whistle.

The game was eventually decided in 17 second-half minutes with goals from Gary Jones corners scored by Andrew Davies and Nahki Wells. The result was City's first League Two away win of the season and, in truth, they were always in command. It had only been a matter of time before the goals they deserved arrived.

There had been crowds in excess of 9,000 for the opening League Two games at Valley Parade. But it was no real surprise when under half that many turned up on Tuesday 25 September for the League Cup third-round clash with Burton Albion.

'All Pay': two words that did more than most to ensure a decent number of stay-aways even if round four beckoned. Well, it did until Burton opened up a two-goal lead within half an hour of kick-off, leaving City staring defeat squarely in the face.

But a triple second-half substitution galvanised the team and the crowd. Nahki Wells bagged a late double and Stephen Darby, a player who went quietly about his business all season long at right back, fired home from distance for a second extra-time win in the competition.

It was pretty breathless stuff, but still nothing to suggest that the run was going to be anything massively out of the ordinary.

Twenty-four hours later the players, fans and Press corps were gathered round television sets to see who they would be watching in the last 16. One of the big boys, perhaps? Or a winnable home game?

In the end it was neither. Premier League minnows Wigan Athletic, a side whose trademark was stylish football, was the name out of the bag, meaning a trip to the DW Stadium to face a side whose rise through the divisions had pretty much mirrored City's slide down.

The initial sense of disappointment was soon lifted, though, as news emerged that fans had snapped up 5,000 tickets for the game. But there was a month to wait and plenty of league points to play for before attentions could turn to the claiming of a top-flight scalp.

City had so far found it tough to lift themselves after

knock-out games, but they were optimistic that trend could be reversed in a top-of-the-table clash with Port Vale.

A 100 per cent home record meant the players were full of confidence, while Parkinson's six-change rule - not really a rule, more of a rotation policy - ensured freshness. Fans believed it would be more of the same at Valley Parade.

They had not, however, counted on that old sporting phenomenon, the smash and grab raid, which saw Vale triumph. Vale's Stoke-born lifelong fan Tom Pope bagged what proved to be the only goal when he capitalised on the rarest of beasts, a Gary Jones error minutes before the break.

It later emerged that the City skipper had been struggling with a back injury in the previous few games, which explained his weak attempt to head the ball towards his back four, which allowed Pope in.

It was also Jones's last appearance before a six-match absence, as he battled to return to fitness.

That was a shame for the veteran who would have earmarked City's next game - against his former club Rochdale - when the 2012-13 fixtures were released.

League Two
September 1 - Rotherham (A) L 0-4
Duke, Meredith, Davies, Oliver, McArdle, Reid, Jones, Doyle (Thompson 70), Hanson, Hines (Atkinson 46), Wells (Connell 75). Unused substitutes: McLaughlin, Darby, McHugh, Hannah.
Referee: Brown. Attendance: 11,199

A head start: Luke Oliver clears *Gary Chadwick*

League Two

September 8 - Accrington Stanley (A) D 1-1

City scorer: Connell 83

McLaughlin, Darby (McArdle 67), Meredith, Davies, Oliver, Reid, Atkinson, Jones, Doyle (Connell 77), Hanson, Hines (Thompson 66). Unused substitutes: Duke, McHugh, Brown, Hannah

Referee: Kettle. Attendance: 3,010

League Two

September 15 - Barnet (H) W 3-0

City scorers: Hanson 47; Connell 55; Davies 57

McLaughlin, McArdle, Davies, Oliver, Meredith, Hines, Jones, Doyle (Atkinson 81), Reid (Thompson 81), Hanson, Connell (Wells 70). Unused substitutes: Duke, Darby, Ravenhill, McHugh.

Referee: Lewis. Attendance: 9,566

League Two
September 18 - Morecambe (H) W 3-1
City scorers: Hanson 44; Reid 80; Jones 87
McLaughlin (Duke 88), McArdle, Davies, Oliver, Meredith, Hines (Atkinson 72), Jones, Doyle, Reid, Hanson, Connell (Wells 68). Unused substitutes: Thompson, Hines, Ravenhill, Darby, McHugh.
Referee: Webb. Attendance: 9,054

League Two
September 22 - Oxford (A) W 2-0
City scorers: Davies 52; Wells 67
McLaughlin, McArdle, Davies, Oliver, Meredith, Reid (Hines 82), Jones, Doyle, Atkinson, Wells (Thompson 68), Hanson. Unused substitutes: Duke, Darby, Ravenhill, Connell, McHugh.
Referee: Davies. Attendance: 6,032

League Cup - Third Round
September 25 - Burton Albion (H) W 3-2 (*after extra-time*)
City scorers: Wells 83, 90; Darby 115
Duke, Darby, Meredith, Davies, McArdle, Ravenhill (Reid 61), Thompson, Atkinson, Jones, Connell (Hanson 61). Hines (Wells 61). Unused substitutes: McLaughlin, Oliver, McHugh, Doyle.
Referee: Miller. Attendance: 4,178

League Two
September 29 - Port Vale (H) L 0-1
McLaughlin, Meredith, Davies, Oliver (Connell 80), McArdle, Reid (Thompson 87), Atkinson (Hines 62), Jones, Doyle, Hanson, Wells. Unused substitutes: Duke, Darby, McHugh, Ravenhill
Referee: Tierney. Attendance: 11,030

League Two				30 September 2012
		P	*GD*	*Pts*
1	Gillingham	9	12	22
2	Port Vale	9	11	19
3	Fleetwood	9	6	17
4	Accrington	9	4	17
5	Exeter	9	5	16
6	**Bradford**	9	5	16
7	Rochdale	9	2	15
8	Cheltenham	9	1	15
9	Burton Albion	9	4	14
10	Rotherham	9	4	14
11	Southend	9	2	14
12	York	9	2	13
13	Northampton	9	2	13
14	Chesterfield	9	2	12
15	Torquay	9	2	12
16	Plymouth	9	-3	10
17	Oxford Utd	9	-8	9
18	Morecambe	9	-5	8
19	Aldershot	9	-5	8
20	Dag & Red	9	-3	7
21	Bristol Rovers	8	-8	7
22	Wimbledon	9	-11	7
23	Wycombe	8	-7	4
24	Barnet	9	-14	2

Not Without Incident

"...It's been a long time coming... #whatgoesaroundcomesaround..."

There was no hint from Phil Parkinson in the build-up to the Tuesday night match at Rochdale that his captain would be missing. But Gary Jones had given the game away himself on the eve of the fixture.

Jones had been due to be presented with something to commemorate his club record 464 appearances for Dale prior to kick-off. However, he had been in contact with the Rochdale Supporters' Trust to say he would not be playing.

In the Twitter era, the veteran had been caught out by a phone call.

Very 'old school'!

The first game of October, without Jones even arriving in Rochdale, ended goalless but it was not without incident.

The first was an injury to in-form Kyel Reid, who would not reappear until mid-December.

The home side were then reduced to ten men before

the break after Bobby Grant's crude challenge on Rory McArdle.

City were always on top but lacked the guile to get through the massed ranks of the Dale defence.

The only cunning came in stoppage time at the end of 90 minutes when a fox emerged from the home end. Having swerved past a startled Andrew Davies it disappeared into the far corner of Spotland.

My first encounter with assistant manager Steve Parkin, who fronted the post-match Press conference, was a positive one despite the result, with the performance enough to maintain the squad's spirits.

One thing you can be certain of in League Two is a lengthy away day - and Dagenham & Redbridge is right up there with the longest.

There is nothing quite like a four-hour journey to focus the mind.

Unfortunately for those fans travelling to the East End, the team produced as bad a first 45 minutes of football as you could wish to see.

The last two performances against Vale and Dale had been decent enough, even if the results had not quite matched them. But the Daggers, struggling at the wrong end of the table, were 2-0 up at the break, had a three-goal advantage by the 51st minute and it could have been far, far worse.

There were City players who appeared not to be relishing the battle.

Wells scored twice in six minutes to give the Bantams hope, but by the time Connell struck near the end it was firmly in the consolation category as the home side had already secured the points with their fourth.

One point from three matches was hardly promotion form and City found themselves back out of the play-off places as the second of the knock-out campaigns began at League One strugglers Hartlepool United.

City's first game in the Johnstone's Paint Trophy was accompanied by a stiff easterly coming in off the North Sea.

Regulars on the east coast might have called it brisk, nothing more than a chilly breeze. But those in the Press box were feeling it and all were delighted that the game kicked off earlier than a league encounter might have done.

Drab would be the kindest way to describe the 90 minutes of football between a City side showing its customary cup changes - including a first rest of the season for Rory McArdle - and a Pools outfit well on its way to becoming embroiled in what would end up being a losing relegation scrap.

The good news for everyone - apart from the early kick-off - was that the JPT goes straight to penalties at the end of 90 minutes. And Bradford had won their previous five shoot outs in all competitions, so it was no surprise when they went through 3-2.

The deciding penalty in this Northern Section second round clash was a peculiar affair and led to one of the longest waits for a decision anyone could remember.

Evan Horwood had to score to keep his side in the tie and struck the ball well. But it thumped into Jon McLaughlin, looped into the air, bounced onto the bar, came down and span away from goal.

The City keeper was sprawled on the floor and unsure what had happened behind him.

And the pause that followed lasted almost as long as the shoot out before referee Graham Salisbury eventually signalled the end of the game - and the start of the City celebrations.

There had been seasons when Bradford had not even

Not this time: Kyel Reid's free-kick hits the bar Gary Chadwick

played four cup ties, let alone won four and, remarkably, the FA Cup had not even started.

Not even a circuitous route home thanks to an A1 closure could dampen spirits.

But it was the league that remained in Parkinson's sights, having built a squad that no matter what it lacked in depth was full of quality.

And there were successive home games to focus on - and a couple of tricky away games as well - before the League Cup fourth-round trip to Wigan.

York City's first visit to Valley Parade for 16 years on Saturday 13 October is not one that will live long in the memory. But it was graced with a special goal involving two of the players added to the squad over the summer.

James Meredith, an Aussie who had appeared in both of York City's games at Wembley the previous season as they won the FA Trophy and promotion from the Conference, was the target of abuse from visiting supporters all afternoon.

He went past three men before finding Zavon Hines on the edge of the area and, two more beaten defenders later, he slammed home his first-ever goal for the Bantams.

The goal equalised an Ashley Chambers strike and the 1-1 result meant Bradford had not won in four games in the league.

They needed to change that seven days later against a Cheltenham side that had not lost on its travels and were flying high in League Two.

Parkinson was unhappy with the visitors' spoiling tactics and his mood can hardly have been lightened when his side went behind from the penalty spot.

But a Wells double, taking his tally for the season to nine, and a magnificent solo effort from Meredith, who in many people's eyes was rapidly becoming the signing of the summer, saw Bradford home 3-1 and back into the top five. One of those Wells scores was also a penalty after Sido Jombati handled the ball in the area, his other a close-range effort from a Hines cross-goal header.

Parkinson, who handed a debut to the first of the campaign's loan signings, Craig Forsyth, was delighted, commenting: 'It was one of our best results of the season.'

One of our best results of the season so far might have been more appropriate in retrospect.

But the City boss would have had to have been a mind reader to know this win would pale into insignificance over the coming weeks.

The wait for the Wigan game was becoming almost intolerable, but there were still trips to Northampton and Burton in the league to negotiate before getting the map out for the journey to Lancashire.

Not many grounds boast a view of a building constructed solely to test lifts.

In fact, Sixfields may be unique in that respect with the National Lift Tower dominating the view from the main stand. At almost 420 feet it is difficult to miss. Difficult except when the fog descends and that was the case when City arrived in Northampton for a Tuesday night clash with the Cobblers.

The nose in front of your face was about as far as you could see at times on the M1 on the way down and there were fears that it could be a wasted journey.

But the weather relented ahead of kick off and Wells' tenth goal of a productive campaign after the break was a sight for sore eyes as it decided the contest.

Football's ludicrous rules were also tested by the Bermudian's celebration after the ball hit the back of the net. Having bagged a hat-trick in the previous season's game at the ground, he wheeled away and ran to the city fans behind the goal, at no stage crossing the advertising boards.

But it was still 'wild' enough for him to pick up a fifth caution for the season, meaning he would miss the trip to Burton four days later.

It was a blow at the time, but turned into a blessing for the striker who missed possibly the coldest day in Staffordshire in living memory.

The wind inside the Pirelli Stadium was bitingly cold - a real three-fleecer.

It was so cold that BBC summariser Graham Mitchell refused to come out of the Press room until contractually obliged to do so - and no one blamed him. He was a shrewd judge as the game did little to warm the City fans, with a Calvin Zola goal giving the Brewers the spoils.

The result was bad, but that was only the half of it.

Ricky Ravenhill clashed with Lee Bell and former top flight and FIFA referee Andy D'Urso felt the City skipper had been overly aggressive and produced a red card.

The Burton man later tweeted: 'Went down like a girl very poor from me! But its been a long time coming!! #whatgoesaroundcomesaround.'

It was the kind of comment that might have got a higher profile player into a deal of trouble.

This being League Two it was noted by the City fans and few others, although the words would come back to haunt Bell as the campaign reached its climax.

The game itself got worse for City after Ravenhill's dismissal as Luke Oliver was helped from the field with what proved to be a season-ending injury.

And fellow central defender Andrew Davies, limping at the end of the opening 45 minutes, failed to re-appear for the second half as he also succumbed to injury.

Three days before the trip to Wigan, City had lost a big player in the middle of the park - he had stepped up to the plate when injury sidelined Gary Jones - and their two main central defenders.

Hardly ideal.

League Two
October 2 - Rochdale (A) D 0-0
McLaughlin; McArdle, Davies, Oliver, Meredith; Reid (Hines 26), Ravenhill (Thompson 75), Doyle, Atkinson; Wells (Connell 81), Hanson. Unused substitutes: Duke, R Jones, Darby, McHugh.
Referee: Adcock. Attendance: 3,461

League Two
October 6 - Dagenham & Redbridge (A) L 3-4
City scorers: Wells 55, 61 (pen); Connell 84
McLaughlin; McArdle, Davies, Oliver, Meredith; Hines (Connell 46), Ravenhill, Doyle, Atkinson (Thompson 72); Wells, Hanson. Unused substitutes: Duke, R Jones, Darby, McHugh, Baker.
Referee: Gibbs. Attendance: 1,768

Football League Trophy - Northern Section - Second Round
October 9 - Hartlepool United (A) D 0-0 (*won 3-2 on pens*)
McLaughlin; Darby, McHugh (Meredith 73), McArdle, Davies; Ravenhill, R Jones (Doyle 68), Atkinson; Connell, Thompson. Hanson (Wells 68). Unused substitutes: Duke, Hines
Referee: G Salisbury. Attendance: 1,777

League Two
October 13 - York City (H) D 1-1
City scorer: Hines 59
McLaughlin, Darby, Meredith, Davies, Oliver, Ravenhill (Hines 57), Atkinson, Doyle, Connell (Thompson 56), Hanson, Wells. Unused substitutes: Duke, McHugh, Jones, Brown, Baker
Referee: Heywood. Attendance: 11,883

League Two
October 20 - Cheltenham Town (H) W 3-1
City scorers: Wells 45 (pen), 68; Meredith 83
McLaughlin, Meredith, Davies, Oliver, McArdle, Ravenhill, Thompson (Atkinson 62), Forsyth (Hines 61), Doyle, Hanson, Wells. Unused substitutes: Duke, Darby, McHugh, Jones, Connell
Referee: Malone. Attendance: 9,648

League Two
October 23 - Northampton (A) W 1-0
City scorer: Wells 53
McLaughlin; McArdle, Meredith, Davies Oliver; Thompson, Ravenhill, Doyle, Forsyth (Atkinson 78); Hanson, Wells. Unused substitutes: Duke, Darby, R Jones, McHugh, Connell, Hines.
Referee: Scott. Attendance: 3,541

League Two
October 27 - Burton Albion (A) L 0-1
McLaughlin; McArdle, Davies (McHugh 46), Oliver (Darby 36), Meredith; Thompson, Doyle, Ravenhill, Forsyth; Connell (G Jones 36), Hanson. Unused substitutes: R Jones, Duke, Atkinson, Hines.
Referee: D'Urso. Attendance: 2,791

League Two				31 October 2012
		P	*GD*	*Pts*
1	Gillingham	15	20	35
2	Port Vale	15	17	30
3	Cheltenham	15	5	28
4	Fleetwood	15	8	26
5	**Bradford**	15	6	24
6	Rotherham	14	6	24
7	Torquay	15	5	24
8	Burton Albion	15	3	23
9	Rochdale	15	2	23
10	York	15	2	22
11	Exeter	15	-3	20
12	Accrington	14	-4	20
13	Southend	15	2	19
14	Northampton	15	-1	19
15	Oxford Utd	15	-5	19
16	Chesterfield	15	-1	18
17	Morecambe	15	-3	18
18	Plymouth	15	-1	17
19	Dag & Red	15	-2	16
20	Bristol Rovers	14	-9	14
21	Wimbledon	15	-11	14
22	Wycombe	14	-10	12
23	Aldershot	15	-13	12
24	Barnet	15	-13	10

Wigan Wonderland

"The 5,000 fans who crossed the Pennines seemed determined to enjoy themselves no matter what..."

Wigan may be an established Premier League side, but that does not necessarily make them attractive cup opposition to teams from the lower leagues.

And the build-up to the game at the DW Stadium was suitably low key.

City were aiming to reach the last eight of the competition for the first time in 24 years.

But there was little national spotlight, no satellite trucks parked in the training ground car park.

In fact it was business as usual at the pre-match Press conference with the usual suspects interviewing - and being interviewed - ahead of the big game.

Parkinson had some real selection problems with Ravenhill, Davies and Oliver all out of contention due to suspension and injury.

It was the biggest test yet of the manager's quality

rather than quantity policy employed when building his squad in the summer.

And, given the problems, the 5,000 fans who crossed the Pennines seemed determined to enjoy themselves no matter what.

The M62 and M6 were as unforgiving as ever and problems on both meant some of the travelling supporters were still in their cars tweeting those inside the ground as kick-off approached.

But those who had won their battle with the motorways made their presence felt.

And when up to their full complement, the City fans made up just under half of the total attendance.

What they witnessed was an impressive display from the Bantams, especially given the players unavailable to the manager.

Rory McArdle, who had operated primarily as a right back to this point, switched to the middle and immediately took on the role of the defence's elder statesman.

And it was his partnership with teenager Carl McHugh that took the eye, with the youngster starting only his third game - the previous two having been at Watford and Hartlepool.

McHugh, along with McArdle, right back Stephen Darby and left back James Meredith, were immense, although they were in danger of being overrun early on.

The warning signs were heeded and wingers Zavon Hines and Garry Thompson retreated to make what was effectively a back six.

Despite the game being something of a rearguard action, City had one of the best chances of the night when Hines raced clear on the right, cut inside and fired in a shot that Ali Al Habsi somehow managed to shovel around the post. Hines slumped to the floor in exhaustion and punched the ground furiously in the knowledge there may not be another opportunity.

He still managed to keep going until the 100th minute of the tie before he eventually crawled from the field.

Whether they are the right way to settle a game or not, there is nothing quite like a penalty shoot-out.

And City's growing reputation from the spot must have filled Wigan's players with dread.

That was certainly the impression they gave.

Nathan Doyle, substitute Gary Jones and Stephen Darby all sent their spot kicks screaming past Al Habsi, while David Jones and Ben Watson were also successful to make it 3-2.

Shaun Maloney sent the ball over the bar, which meant that Wigan had no margin for error after Alan Connell had made it 4-2.

The pressure was well and truly on Jordi Gomez who had failed to hit the target from his side's best chance over two hours of football on the stroke of half-time.

And when Matt Duke saved the Spanish midfielder's kick the celebrations were up and, quite literally, running.

The keeper, arms aloft as he raced towards the touchline, was swamped by teammates; the stand furthest away from the shoot out housing the City fans erupted.

Not since September 1995 when Bradford beat Nottingham Forest in the second round had City knocked a Premier League club out of the League Cup.

And boss Parkinson summed up the mood of everyone in the City camp when he said: 'I am ecstatic.

'I thought the discipline of the team was top drawer. It shows you what can be done with big hearts and discipline and everyone stuck to their jobs.

'The first 15 minutes caught us cold a little bit. We knew what system they would play, the movement was difficult but we worked it out as the game wore on and got better and better.

'We had moments ourselves when we looked like we could create something, especially with Zavon down the right hand side.

'It is a great night for the club and I said to the players in the dressing room that the support we had was the reason everyone has come to Bradford City.

'That level of support was Premiership support and the lads have absolutely lapped it up.

'I can feel the momentum in the city building behind us. There is a lot of positivity in and around the club.

'The lads are elated. It is hard to bring them back down to earth tonight, but I don't really want to. I want them to enjoy it and savour the moment.

'To come to a Premiership club with so many injuries will give you an understanding of what a great win this was for us.'

Quite correctly, he had particular words of praise for shoot-out hero Matt Duke, who had not featured in any of the previous eight games.

'You do feel confident because we have had so many in the past and the lads have always kept cool heads,' said Parkinson after his side's seventh successive shoot-out win.

'The penalties were excellent and I was pleased for Dukey. While he has been out of the team he has been working with Jon [McLaughlin] keeping his professionalism before his moment in the spotlight.'

League Cup - Fourth Round
October 30 - Wigan Athletic (A) D 0-0 (*won 4-2 on pens*)
Duke, Darby, McHugh, McArdle, Meredith, Hines (Baker 101), Thompson (Jones 56), Doyle, Atkinson, Wells (Connell 65), Hanson. Subs not used: McLaughlin, Brown, Bass, Swain.
Referee: East. Attendance: 11,777

City's players were probably just about recovering from their celebrations when, 24 hours after their win at Wigan, the draw for the quarter-finals was made.

With Swansea and Norwich having produced shocks of their own, the nerves were jangling as the balls were pulled out of the bag - and it can't have been any easier for the players and club staff!

Chelsea were the second out, away to Leeds, taking away the possibility - one few relished if they were honest - of a big Yorkshire derby.

Swansea were paired with Middlesbrough and Norwich came out alongside Aston Villa.

It was the big one.

And when City were next out everyone knew they had a home tie with Arsenal.

The spotlight was firmly on Parkinson's side.

'We've always said our time will come and we would get that massive cup tie and it's finally happened,' said an elated Parkinson.

'To see the words Bradford City v Arsenal going across the TV screen was fantastic.

'It's great for the club, great for the two chairmen and great for all the supporters.

'Money-wise, getting an away tie to one of the big

teams would have earned us maybe a bit more. But equally, Arsenal at home with 20,000 of our fans there will be something special - and I'm positive it's going to be on TV.

'As the games were getting played and Norwich and Swansea were winning, the odds were lengthening on us being given a lucrative draw. But it's as good as you are going to get in terms of playing at home to one of the Premiership's biggest clubs.'

Such is Parkinson's professionalism, however, that thoughts turned to the FA Cup tie with Northampton.

And any mention of the A-word over the next couple of weeks would be met with a stoney silence.

Such was the scheduling of the League Cup that City would play ten games before they were able to concentrate on the Gunners.

November Fireworks

"It was a staggering eighth successive penalty shoot-out success..."

First up after the Wigan game was a second trip of the season to Northampton, this time for the first round of the FA Cup.

With Ritchie Jones making just his second appearance of the season and youngster Scott Brown his debut, it was immediately clear where this game lay in Phil Parkinson's list of priorities.

Having been followed by 5,000-plus at Wigan, the fans had also made up their minds about the FA Cup, despite a second chance to marvel at the concrete lift tower.

A less than average 281 made the journey on the first Saturday in November, a handful more than had travelled to Sixfields for a Tuesday evening league game.

One of the trademarks of the season had been that no matter how many changes were made to the starting line-up, the City team always seemed to perform.

Will Atkinson put City ahead from the edge of the area only for former loanee Louis Moult to level just past the hour mark.

The Bantams had chances to finish off the job but could not take them and that meant probably the worst of all outcomes - a replay.

The one bonus was that another midweek game would mean less time to think about you-know-who in the other cup.

Drab hardly does justice to City's first home game since the shoot out win at Wigan, a goalless draw with Chesterfield. Understandably, inside Valley Parade it was flat; very flat for a Tuesday night match, which usually have plenty of atmosphere.

From a City perspective, it was the first real sign that their efforts in cup competitions were starting to take their toll, on the fans as well as the players.

And with neither able to lift the other, the stalemate was almost inevitable.

It did little to lift the spirits and four days later the Bantams faced a trip to lowly Aldershot, a side they had lost to on each of their previous four visits to Hampshire.

Wells was the goal hero yet again, however, bagging a first half double to ensure City kept firmly in touch with the top three and leaving the Shots rooted to the foot of the table. He would have bagged a hat-trick had his second-half bicycle kick not hit the post.

Had it not been in a season of major cup drama, the FA Cup first round replay with Northampton on Tuesday 13 November would have been among the highlights.

At the time it was, but Arsenal were looming and history was still waiting to be made.

It was the third meeting of the campaign with the

Cup priorities: City boss Phil Parkinson made changes *Gintare Karpaviciute*

Cobblers and by some distance the best. Will Atkinson's first half strike was cancelled out by an Ishmel Demontagnac spot-kick as the sides turned round at the break all square.

Nahki Wells then appeared to have won the tie when he scored a penalty in the final minute of normal time.

But big Clive Platt had other ideas as City switched off for a split second and it was extra-time.

When Kelvin Langmead struck it looked like the Bantams were heading out, especially as the game went into added-time at the end of extra-time with City down to ten men, after James Meredith was forced from the field with Phil Parkinson having made all three changes.

But Carl McHugh's first senior goal - a looping header in the first minute of stoppage-time - sent the tie to penalties and everyone knew what that meant.

Even when the shoot-out began with Wells' penalty

being saved by Northampton keeper Shane Higgs, confidence remained high.

Platt put the visitors ahead before Gary Jones opened the Bantams' account. Then Jon McLaughlin saved from Danny East, before Will Atkinson fired Bradford ahead.

Kelvin Langmead missed, allowing Stephen Darby to make it 3-1 and, despite Lewis Hornby converting, Northampton knew their cup future was on the line as Ricky Ravenhill fired City through.

'These lads never know when they are beaten,' said Parkinson - and why would they?

It was a staggering eighth successive penalty shoot-out success and it set up a home tie in round two against Brentford - another game to fit in before the Gunners came to town.

'We've got some record with shoot-outs. You could feel the confidence from the supporters and players,' added Parkinson.

'When you've been in that position a few times, the experience has got to help you.'

The FA Cup tie was the first of three games in a row on home soil with the two that followed it crucial in terms of league promotion.

But City had failed to win any of the five league games they had played following cup victories previously during the season.

And, sadly for them, the game against Exeter extended that poor run as they went down 1-0 and slipped to seventh in the table.

Jamie Cureton, who played with Phil Parkinson at Reading and under him at Colchester, scored the only goal of a game that City did more than enough to get something from.

But Alan Connell had an effort cleared off the line and Nahki Wells had strong claims for a penalty waved away, despite appearing to have been dragged to the floor by Steve Tully.

There was little time to dwell on the disappointment with the Devon theme continuing three days later when Plymouth arrived in town.

And while they won the game 1-0 thanks to a Gary Jones goal, the game was marred by a serious injury to a promising youngster on loan from Sunderland.

John Egan, son of the Kerry Gaelic football star of the same name, was playing just his third game for the Bantams having been drafted in following the problems suffered by Luke Oliver and Andrew Davies at Burton.

And he had shown enough to suggest he would be a useful, albeit temporary, addition to the squad.

But in the 13th minute, with the ball heading for the touchline in front of the main stand, he collapsed to the ground after landing badly.

There is no worse sight on a sporting field than a player going down with no one near him.

And when teammates turn away shaking their heads, as several including skipper Jones did, you know it is serious.

Egan had suffered a season-ending double fracture.

That meant more central defensive problems for Phil Parkinson and his coaching staff.

They had coped before - and would cope again.

But you may have been forgiven for fearing the worst as, within a minute of their next outing at Bristol Rovers, they found themselves trailing.

The fact that it was former Bantam central defender Guy Branston, making his Rovers debut on loan, who powered home the early header for the Gasheads made it even worse.

Push start: James Meredith in the thick of the action as usual *Gary Chadwick*

And throw in that in ten previous games away to Rovers City had never won - at Eastville, Twerton Park or their current Memorial Ground home - the outlook was bleak.

Nahki Wells levelled before Tom Eaves' low drive restored Rovers' lead.

Carl McHugh headed a second City equaliser only for a Michael Smith volley to put Rovers in front for a third time.

The game eventually ended 3-3, with James Hanson heading his first goal since September.

But there was still time for some late drama with both sides being reduced to ten men - incorrectly as it turned out.

City midfielder Nathan Doyle was shown a straight red for his part in a fracas that followed a lunging challenge by Seanan Clucas on James Meredith.

Wayne Brown was also dismissed when he was shown a second yellow card despite the fact he had nothing to do with the challenge or the pushing and shoving that followed it.

Even with the naked eye, the double dismissal looked wrong.

'It was a bad tackle by their player and I was stood right by it all,' said Parkinson immediately after the game.

'There were no punches thrown or any grappling from what I could see and I asked the referee why he had been sent off and he didn't answer me. The fourth official said he'd kicked one of their players, which I certainly didn't see.

'Doyley said he went over and had a go at the lad for the challenge but that he didn't kick him. I think the ref has made a major error there.'

City were quick to lodge an appeal on Doyle's behalf, especially after watching the replays that evening.

The red was subsequently overturned and the midfielder was free to play in City's next game - their eighth cup tie of the campaign at home to Brentford in the first round of the FA Cup.

FA Cup - First Round
November 3 - Northampton (A) D 1-1
City scorer: Atkinson 32
Duke; Darby, Doyle, McHugh, Meredith; Brown, Atkinson, G Jones (McArdle 81), R Jones; Connell (Wells 75), Thompson (Hanson 75). Unused substitutes: McLaughlin, Baker, Hines, Bass.
Referee: Eltringham. Attendance: 2,512

League Two
November 6 - Chesterfield (H) D 0-0
Duke, Darby, McArdle, Egan, Meredith, Hines (Forsyth 82 mins), Doyle, G Jones, Atkinson, Wells, Thompson, (Connell 68mins). Unused substitutes: McLaughlin, Baker, McHugh, R Jones, Brown.
Referee: Attwell. Attendance: 8,841

League Two
November 10 - Aldershot (A) W 2-0
City scorer: Wells 29, 39
Duke; Darby, McArdle, Egan, Meredith; Atkinson, G Jones, Doyle, Forsyth; Wells (Hines 80), Hanson. Unused subs: McLaughlin, Connell, McHugh, Thompson, Ravenhill, Brown.
Referee: Langford. Attendance: 2,143

FA Cup - First Round Replay
November 13 - Northampton (H) D 3-3 (*won 4-2 on pens*)
City scorers: Atkinson 35; Wells 90 (pen); McHugh 120
McLaughlin, Darby, Meredith, McHugh, McArdle, Ravenhill, Atkinson, Brown (Jones 63), Hines (Baker 29), Hanson, Connell (Wells 73). Unused substitutes: Duke, Doyle, Bass, Swain
Referee: Russell. Attendance; 2,951

League Two
November 17 - Exeter City (H) L 0-1
Duke, McHugh, Egan, McArdle, Naylor (Thompson 76), Atkinson, Forsyth (Connell 46), Jones, Doyle, Hanson, Wells. Unused substitutes: McLaughlin, Ravenhill, Brown, Bass, Baker
Referee: Haines. Attendance: 10,434

League Two
November 20 - Plymouth Argyle (H) W 1-0
City scorer: Jones 21
Duke, Darby, Meredith, Egan (McHugh 18), McArdle, Thompson (Jones 80), Atkinson, Jones, Doyle, Hanson, Wells (Connell 77). Unused substitutes: McLaughlin, Naylor, Ravenhill, Forsyth
Referee: Bates. Attendance: 8,843

League Two
November 24 - Bristol Rovers (A) D 3-3
City scorers: Wells 29; McHugh 55; Hanson 67
Duke; Darby, McArdle, McHugh, Meredith; Thompson (R Jones 76), G Jones, Doyle, Atkinson; Wells (Connell 73), Hanson. Unused substitutes: Ravenhill, Forsyth, Naylor, Turgott, McLaughlin.
Referee: Phillips. Attendance: 5,092

League Two		30 November 2012		
		P	*GD*	*Pts*
1	Gillingham	20	20	41
2	Port Vale	20	23	39
3	Cheltenham	20	2	35
4	Southend	20	12	32
5	**Bradford**	20	8	32
6	Fleetwood	20	8	31
7	Rotherham	19	3	31
8	Rochdale	19	2	30
9	Exeter	20	0	30
10	Northampton	20	5	29
11	Burton Albion	20	0	29
12	Chesterfield	20	3	28
13	Torquay	19	3	28
14	Accrington	19	-4	26
15	Dag & Red	19	4	25
16	Morecambe	20	-2	25
17	York	19	-3	24
18	Oxford Utd	20	-6	24
19	Wycombe	19	-9	19
20	Plymouth	20	-7	18
21	Bristol Rovers	19	-14	18
22	Wimbledon	20	-16	18
23	Aldershot	20	-16	17
24	Barnet	20	-16	15

A Spot of Bother

"A technicality in the paperwork meant he should not have made his debut..."

Phil Parkinson made his now customary changes to the side ahead of a Friday night FA Cup second round clash with the League One Brentford.

And the changes included debuts for new loan signings Blair Turgott and Curtis Good.

Highly-rated West Ham youngster Turgott and Newcastle United's Australian centre-back Good were brought in to bolster a squad still battling on four fronts.

And the fact they were available for all cup competitions having not been involved in their parent clubs' senior squads was key.

Both acquitted themselves well, Turgott showing some neat trickery on the wing, Good defending well and displaying an array of long-range passing from the back.

James Hanson was on target to cancel out Clayton Donaldson's opener and the new boys' arrivals were proved

Jump to it: Nahki Wells evades a sliding tackle *Gary Chadwick*

spot on as City had yet another game to fit in. Both also played in the Johnstone's Paint Trophy tie at Port Vale four days later, in which Garry Thompson laid on goals for Craig Forsyth and Ritchie Jones as the Bantams progressed 2-0.

Then came the news that they had been thrown out of the FA Cup, as Good had not been eligible to play.

A technicality in the paperwork meant he should not have made his debut.

Given the hectic programme of matches City were involved in, the club could have been forgiven for accepting the punishment and moving on.

Even Phil Parkinson admitted: 'We have a lot of games coming up, so if we are out of it will take it on the chin and move on. But if we are in it, we will go to Brentford and give it our best.'

In any case, City had a home league game with Torquay to focus on before Arsenal arrived in the Capital One Cup.

As hors d'oeuvres for big cup ties go, Torquay are very disappointing.

But, as Parkinson kept insisting, the league remained the major focus and three points were a must.

The overriding memory of the game against the Gulls was the display of their keeper Michael Poke, who pulled off a string of saves to deny City.

But the Bantams eventually broke through with five minutes remaining and, fittingly in their final game before facing the Gunners, it was Alan Connell who fired home the only goal.

Connell is from Islington, his family are all big Arsenal fans and he used to wear the red and white when he was a youngster on the books of north London rivals Tottenham. He had even been to see his side play in a couple of away games earlier in the season.

But in the aftermath of his crucial goal - one that sent City to a season-equalling high of fourth in the table - he did not know whether it was enough to earn him a place in the starting line-up to face the team he supports.

He would, however, play his part in the extraordinary events of a truly memorable Tuesday night in December.

FA Cup Second Round
November 30 - Brentford (H) D 1-1
City scorer: Hanson 70
Duke, Darby, Meredith, McArdle, Good, Ravenhill (G Jones 61), Thompson (Atkinson 61), Doyle, Turgott, Hanson, Connell (Wells 61). Unused substitutes: McLaughlin, McHugh, R Jones, Baker
Referee: Sutton. Attendance: 3,620

Football League Trophy - Northern Section - Quarter-final
December 4 - Port Vale (A) W 2-0
City scorers: R Jones 46; Forysth 55
McLaughlin, Darby (Doyle 62), Naylor, Good, McHugh, Turgott (G Jones 62), Ravenhill, R Jones, Forsyth, Thompson (Hanson 72), Connell. Unused substitutes: Duke, Wells.
Referee: Drysdale. Attendance: 2,786

League Two
December 8 - Torquay United (H) W 1-0
City scorer: Connell 85
Duke, Darby, Meredith, McHugh (Connell 80), McArdle, Thompson (Turgott 62), Atkinson, Jones, Doyle, Hanson, Wells (Naylor 89). Unused substitutes: McLaughlin, Ravenhill, Jones, Forsyth
Referee: Bond. Attendance: 9,347

Gunning for Arsenal

"Everyone wanted a piece of the Bantams - and they were happy to give it..."

Lights. Cameras. Action. Had you just arrived from outer space at Apperley Bridge the day before the Arsenal game you would have known immediately that something was happening.

Most pre-match Press conferences involved a quartet of local media outlets and a player in addition to boss Phil Parkinson.

But on Tuesday 11 December, there was a real buzz about the place. Everyone wanted a piece of the Bantams - and they were happy to give it.

After all, this was their day in the spotlight; a day unlikely to be repeated any time soon.

There was, not surprisingly, a completely different feel to match-night as well.

Security was ramped up with 4,500 Arsenal fans expected to fill the Midland Road stand at Valley Parade.

Roads were shut three hours before kick-off and the car park behind the Kop was filled with satellite-topped TV trucks.

The eyes of the footballing world were on Bradford.

Could they deliver?

There was a buzz of excitement inside the Press lounge pre-match, although excitement made way for trepidation when news of the strength of the Arsenal side started to leak out.

Szczesny, Sagna, Mertesacker, Vermaelen, Gibbs, Wilshere, Ramsey, Cazorla, Coquelin, Podolski, Gervinho.

Household names and recognisable faces wherever you looked.

Surely City had no chance against this side, but the atmosphere inside Valley Parade was special.

There was a sense of expectation, tempered with realism. And, in any case, this was the reward for wins over Notts County, Burton Albion and Wigan Athletic.

It was the culmination of a great run, a night to remember, something to tell the grandchildren about.

Not surprisingly given the standard of opposition - 65 places separated the sides in the league pyramid - City were on the back foot in the opening stages, as Thomas Vermaelen and Lukas Podolski failed to make the most of decent chances.

Then it happened; City scored.

Nahki Wells was brought down.

Gary Jones raised his finger to the skies and sent over the free-kick.

Will Atkinson flicked the ball on and Garry Thompson was at the back post to smack it home.

The majority of a 23,971 crowd inside Valley Parade - and, if we are being honest here, a section of the Press box -

went wild. Only 16 minutes had been played and the Bantams faithful were in fantasy land.

Francis Coquelin beat Matt Duke, but not the post, and Gervinho somehow failed to connect with a Kieran Gibbs cross when it seemed inevitable he would slide home an equaliser from a couple of yards.

Wells trickled an effort a foot wide of the target - many thought it was rolling in - in a show of defiance on the stroke of half-time.

Not until the 68th minute did Arsenal manage to get a shot on target.

Once they did, they forced Duke into a number of fine saves, the big man standing firm as the efforts took their toll on his teammates, who were playing the game from memory having run themselves into the ground.

For all the visitors' class and silky skills, it was an old-fashioned League Two goal that eventually saw them draw level with two minutes remaining.

And when Vermaelen headed home Santi Cazorla's left-wing cross the City dream appeared over.

Cazorla struck the bar in 30 agonising minutes of extra-time, but the Bantams somehow survived and that meant they had a crack at extending their remarkable shoot-out winning record which stood at eight going into the tie.

Nathan Doyle strode forward purposefully and smacked his penalty into the back of the net, although Wojciech Szczesny managed to get his hand to the ball.

Then Carzorla was denied by a fine save from Matt Duke, the keeper diving to his left to save and give City the edge.

When skipper Gary Jones followed Doyle's lead the dream was alive again.

Marouane Chamakh lacked conviction in his

Come on, City: The fans lapped up a surprise victory over Arsenal *Gintare Karpaviciute*

approach to the spot and saw his effort come back off the post. But Stephen Darby was tentative and that allowed Szczesny to make a simple save to his left.

Jack Wilshire, Arsenal's best player over two hours, sent Duke the wrong way.

Alan Connell, who had replaced Wells with 16 minutes of the 90 remaining, then ensured City kept their noses firmly in front.

The Arsenal fan did not celebrate but did allow himself a smile as he walked back to his ecstatic teammates in the centre circle.

Alex Oxlade-Chamberlain had to score to keep the shoot out going - and he did.

And when Ritchie Jones's placed effort was saved the City fans were left wondering whether the chance had gone.

Arsenal skipper Vermaelen, whose goal had earned his side the lifeline, sent Cool Hand Duke the wrong way and time seemed to stand still.

The keeper turned his head, watching as the ball rolled goalwards only to see it strike the base of the post and rebound to safety.

Cue the celebrations.

The players raced to Duke, they were mobbed by jubilant fans, City legend John Hendrie summed it all up with an on-air cry of: 'You Beauty'.

Valley Parade had not seen anything like it for many years. And, as everyone of a City persuasion leapt for joy, they all knew it would take time for it to truly sink in.

It was scarcely believable.

'Arsene [Wenger] said he was going to bring a strong team but we were still surprised by just how strong it was,' admitted Phil Parkinson. 'He knew we were a good side.

'Matt Duke pulled off some crucial saves in what was a difficult night for goalkeepers, but the defenders protected him terrifically.'

It was a British record ninth successive penalty shoot out win for the Bantams.

But Parkinson was keen that did not detract from his side's performance over 120 minutes.

'The talk might be about the penalty shoot-out but I want the talk to be about the overall performance,' he said.

'We were three minutes away from beating Arsenal, who played their strongest team.

'What a performance the lads put in.'

From a personal point of view, Parkinson added that it was one of the best nights of his managerial career.

'It has got to be up there with the very best,' he said.

'One of their players probably earns more than our whole budget - and that is probably one of the reserve players as well.

'To beat Arsenal in front of a packed house, it doesn't get much better than that.

'I am so pleased for the people of Bradford. We want to put Bradford back on the map and I think we are starting to do that.'

The win was also good news for the club accountants with a two-legged semi final to come in January.

'It has secured our long-term future,' said City's Director of Operations David Baldwin.

'Two televised ties will bring the club in an extra £1 million in revenue.'

One of the big follow-up stories to emerge from the Arsenal game was Gary Jones claiming that Torquay gave City more of a game than the Gunners.

On the pitch, Jones was 'lost for words' when asked what the result meant to him and his teammates.

As the celebrations had started to die down he spoke to a section of the national Press at the back of the main stand.

'I think Torquay gave us a tougher game,' he told reporters. 'The lads were unbelievable.

'It was like a role reversal, because Torquay defended really well against us, whereas it was us defending really well against Arsenal.

'We defended really well and our organisation and discipline were really good, which set us in good stead.

'To beat a full-strength Arsenal in the Capital One Cup quarter-final is what dreams are made of and what you play football for.

'Without a shadow of a doubt Arsenal should be

Spot on: Nathan Doyle coolly slotted home in the shoot out *Gintare Karpaviciute*

embarrassed. No disrespect to us and our lads, but they should be beating Bradford City.'

The spotlight remained on City the following day, with Parkinson tracked down on a family shopping trip in York and revealing that the win had been the lead sports news story in Australia.

The club would have to wait a further seven days to discover who they would play next.

League Cup - Quarter-final
December 11 - Arsenal (H) D 1-1 (*won 3-2 on pens*)
City scorer: Thompson 16
Duke, Darby, McArdle, McHugh, Meredith, Thompson (Jones 72), Doyle, Jones, Atkinson (Turgot 92), Wells (Connell 74), Hanson. Unused substitutes: McLaughlin, Ravenhill, Hines, Good.
Referee: Dean. Attendance: 23,971

City's penalty shoot-out run:

- *6 October 2009:* Johnstone's Paint Trophy - Notts County (H)
- *10 November 2009:* Johnstone's Paint Trophy - Port Vale (H)
- *30 August 2011:* Johnstone's Paint Trophy - Sheffield Wednesday (A)
- *4 October 2011:* Johnstone's Paint Trophy - Huddersfield (A)
- *8 November 2011:* Johnstone's Paint Trophy - Sheffield United (A)
- *9 October 2012:* Johnstone's Paint Trophy - Hartlepool (A)
- *30 October 2012:* Capital One Cup - Wigan (A)
- *13 November 2012:* FA Cup - Northampton (H)
- *11 December 2012:* Capital One Cup - Arsenal (H)

Scrappy Christmas

"Essex in December is not usually at the top of potential weekend break destinations..."

The day after they had knocked Arsenal out of one competition Bradford City were reinstated in another as they won their appeal against expulsion from the FA Cup.

Football chiefs said it had been a genuine mistake and that there had been no attempt to deceive anyone.

Newcastle United had given verbal permission for Curtis Good to play in the competition, but that was not forwarded in writing to the relevant authorities. And it emerged it was City who had pointed out the error.

It was good news for the Bantams but meant another game, this time in west London, days before Christmas.

Before that they had to return to league action and see how their exertions against Arsenal would affect them at Southend United.

Essex in December is not usually at the top of potential weekend break destinations.

But the Bantams and a couple of hundred fans headed south looking to maintain their promotion challenge.

The first surprise on arrival was how mild it was given the frosty conditions City had endured four days earlier.

And there were plenty of locals keen to discuss the midweek cup clash with the Gunners.

But Phil Parkinson knew his side had a job to do and, against a Southend side whose manager Paul Sturrock had just been awarded manager of the month for November, named the same team that had grabbed the headlines.

All was going well as Nahki Wells and a comedy own goal from Luke Prosser - is there a better sight that seeing an opposition defender slice the ball into the roof of his own net? - gave City a comfortable lead.

But the Bantams began to run out of energy - mental as much as physical - as the game went on and the home side forced their way back.

Ryan Creswell pulled one back with ten minutes remaining then, with the seconds ticking away, a long ball down the middle undid the Bantams and Gavin Tomlin stole in to level.

Parkinson was bristling in his post-match interviews, although his disappointment was tempered by the reality that it had been a major test for his players after their knockout exploits.

'After what we have gone through in terms of the euphoria of Tuesday night, to come to Southend and be 2-0 up against a team which is up and around us in the top seven was a magnificent display,' said Parkinson.

'The players put themselves on the line for the club. It was a hard ask and I thought they were great.

'There is a tinge of disappointment because we want

to win every game but, let's be fair, we couldn't have asked for any more could we?'

They were back in cup action again at Brentford seven days after the Arsenal game, but only two players - Carl McHugh and Rory McArdle - started both ties.

City had earned their replay at Griffin Park thanks to a 1-1 draw at Valley Parade and that successful appeal against expulsion from the competition.

And given the lengths to which they had gone to ensure their continuing participation, it may have appeared strange that Phil Parkinson made nine changes to his starting line-up.

He might have made 11 but for the long-term injuries to Andrew Davies and Luke Oliver and the fact that neither Tom Naylor nor Curtis Good, whose inclusion in the first game had been the cause of the initial expulsion, were available to him.

Kyel Reid appeared for the first time since October and Forayah Bass made his first ever start for the senior side.

Reid made a major impact as he fired City in front 11 minutes before the break.

Marcello Trotta levelled from the spot - if only he had managed to score from 12 yards against Doncaster on the final day of the League One campaign - before Alan Connell put the Bantams ahead for the second time four minutes into extra-time.

The seemingly impossible was becoming a distinct possibility.

But Brentford had other ideas and after Trotta's second made it 2-2, Clayton Donaldson and Harry Forrester goals saw the Bees home.

Parkinson had cleared his selection with the City hierarchy and was pleased with how they performed.

'I thought it was a gallant performance from the lads, given the team we had out, I don't think we could have asked for much more,' he said.

'We didn't want to go to extra-time, but there are a lot of benefits from the game.

'We decided with the board that we would leave some of our key players back in Bradford for the game, because some of them really needed a rest.'

City had got to December 18 without losing a single cup tie - and the game in west London was their 11th of the campaign in knock-out competitions.

That would be no mean feat in any season, but there was so much more still to come.

The day after the Brentford game, the Capital One Cup semi-final line-up was completed when Chelsea thrashed Leeds 5-1 at Elland Road.

And fans everywhere gathered round their TVs to see who the Bantams would get in the last four.

Chelsea and Swansea came out together first and when Bradford were the third side drawn they knew it would be Aston Villa over two legs, with the first at Valley Parade.

Just 24 hours after City's FA Cup exit, cup fever was back, but this time it was one tie from Wembley and the whole dynamic would change.

In the build up to the game against Arsenal - and it was a six-week wait between the win at Wigan and the game with the gunners - City had managed to hold their form well.

Phil Parkinson had somehow managed to focus his players' minds so well that they won five and drew four of the ten matches they played between the ties against Premier League opposition.

The question was could he do it again?

There was no immediate chance to tell as the game at

Wycombe Wanderers was postponed. In a grand gesture to the fans, City's board bought 2,000 tickets for the December 22 game at Adams Park and also offered transport to Buckinghamshire for just £10.

And the majority of those who took up the offer must have feared the worst as they made their way down the M1 with the rain becoming increasingly torrential.

News came through of a planned pitch inspection but the fans kept going.

Most had got at least as far as Northampton when the word came through that the surface was in no state to host a match and they turned round and trudged back to West Yorkshire.

London Wasps and Sale Sharks managed to play a televised Aviva Premiership game at the same venue 24 hours later, but for City supporters there was no more football until after Christmas.

The first of the Festive games was a less than glamorous game against Accrington Stanley, a side City had been unable to beat at Valley Parade in ten games stretching back to 1955.

City went ahead when Garry Thompson slotted home a James Hanson knock-down but, despite having Dean Winnard sent off midway through the second half, Stanley levelled when Romuald Boco fired home.

City fans were resigned to their poor home run against the Lancastrians continuing until Alan Connell popped up to head home a Kyel Reid cross with four minutes remaining.

Victory kept Bradford fifth, just three points from the automatic promotion places.

Ordinarily, the Christmas and New Year period is the busiest any footballer will be faced with.

But the Accrington game was the Bantams' 34th of the campaign and the players and fans were used to a heavy workload.

The final match of 2012 was at home to Rochdale, a side that had hung on gamely with ten men for a goalless draw when the sides met at Spotland in October.

Dale boss John Coleman may have been a little over the top in comparing his side to Barcelona after their 4-2 win.

But they were too good on the day for Bradford who should have held onto possession far better.

It was a strange game in which all six goals came before half-time, Alan Connell scoring both for City.

And the second 11,000-plus crowd for a home game in the league were left scratching their collective heads as City's run of five League Two games without defeat came to a shuddering halt.

There were two away games before the first leg of the Capital One Cup against Villa. How would they fare?

League Two
December 15 - Southend United (A) D 2-2
City scorers: Wells 28; Prosser 55 (og)
Duke, Darby, Meredith, McHugh, McArdle, G Jones, Doyle (Ravenhill 81), Atkinson, Thompson (Forsyth 57), Wells (Hines 70), Hanson. Unused substitutes: McLaughlin, Connell, Turgott, Good
Referee: Martin. Attendance: 5,142

FA Cup Second Round Replay
December 18 - Brentford (A) L 2-4 (*after extra-time*)
City scorers: Reid 34; Connell 94 pen
McLaughlin; R Jones, Bass (Curtis 105), McArdle, McHugh; Brown, Ravenhill, Reid (Thompson 56), Turgott; Connell, Hines (Baker 67). Unused substitutes: Darby, Hepworth, Erangey, Duke
Referee: G Scott. Attendance: 2,643

League Two
December 26 - Accrington Stanley (H) W 2-1
City scorers: Thompson 24; Connell 86
Duke, Darby, Meredith, McArdle, Naylor, Thompson, Atkinson (Reid 81), G Jones, Doyle, Hanson, Hines (Wells 44). Unused substitutes: McHugh, Ravenhill, R Jones, Turgott, Connell
Referee: Eltringham. Attendance: 11,181

League Two
December 29 - Rochdale (H) L 2-4
City scorers: Connell 19 (pen), 36 (pen)
Duke, Darby, Meredith, McArdle, Naylor (Hannah 74), Reid, Thompson (Atkinson 46), G Jones, Doyle (Turgott 74), Hanson, Connell. Unused substitutes: McLaughlin, Ravenhill, R Jones, Hines
Referee: Coote. Attendance: 11,198

League Two		31 December 2012		
		P	*GD*	*Pts*
1	Port Vale	24	23	46
2	Gillingham	23	20	45
3	Cheltenham	24	4	42
4	Southend	25	16	40
5	Rotherham	24	6	40
6	**Bradford**	24	8	39
7	Burton Albion	25	3	39
8	Fleetwood	24	9	37
9	Chesterfield	25	5	36
10	Rochdale	25	2	36
11	Exeter	24	-1	35
12	Northampton	23	6	33
13	Torquay	23	3	33
14	Oxford Utd	24	-1	32
15	Dag & Red	24	1	31
16	York	24	-4	31
17	Wycombe	24	-8	29
18	Morecambe	24	-3	28
19	Accrington	25	-12	27
20	Plymouth	25	-6	24
21	Barnet	25	-15	23
22	Aldershot	24	-16	22
23	Bristol Rovers	23	-20	19
24	Wimbledon	23	-20	19

Scrappier New Year

"City's players were a tight-knit group, ready to battle to the last bfreath for each other..."

As a cobweb blowing away exercise, a New Year's Day trip to Morecambe really fits the bill.

The main stand at the Globe Arena is substantially higher than the other three sides and, as a consequence, the biting wind coming off the Irish Sea goes straight through anyone sitting in it.

James Hanson had a great chance to secure all three points but was unable to convert as the game ended goalless and Bradford slipped a place to seventh.

Struggling Barnet, under former Holland star Edgar Davids, were next up so there was a great chance to get back on track - or so everyone thought.

Almost 500 City fans packed into Underhill's away end and all watched in disbelief as the home side took the spoils thanks to goals from Taiwo Atieno and John Oster.

The disbelief came as a result of City having a

remarkable 21 attempts on goal without being able to break through.

And Phil Parkinson was as puzzled as the supporters by the result. 'We dominated the game from start to finish,' he said. 'The effort was there, we just lacked that bit of composure in the final third. For all the attempts we had, I don't think their keeper made too many great saves.

'It was almost as if we were trying too hard. You need a bit of calmness about your play and we lacked that.'

Throw in the fact that, elsewhere, Villa's 2-1 FA Cup win over Ipswich was their first victory for five games and it was hardly the best preparation for the first leg of a cup semi-final. But City's players were a tight-knit group, ready to battle to the last breath for each other. The focus was now on a record breaking third top-flight scalp.

League Two
January 1 - Morecambe ((A) D 0-0
Duke, Darby, McArdle, Doyle, Meredith (Good 46), R Jones, Ravenhill, Atkinson, G Jones (Reid 73), Hines (Wells 46), Hanson. Unused substitutes: McLaughlin, Connell, Naylor, Turgott.
Referee: Lewis. Attendance: 3,635

League Two
January 5 - Barnet (A) L 0-2
Duke, Darby (Turgott 77), McArdle, Doyle, Good, Ravenhill (Connell 66), R Jones (Reid 46), Atkinson, G Jones, Wells, Hanson. Unused substitutes: Hines, Brown, McHugh, McLaughlin
Referee: Heywood. Attendance: 2,317

Above: James Hanson celebrates one of his fifteen goals in a fine season *Gary Chadwick*

Below: The ever-busy Nathan Doyle runs at the York City midfield *Gary Chadwick*

Above: Alan Connell celebrates his goal against Barnet *Gary Chadwick*

Below: Nahki Wells holds up the ball as the defence closes in *Gary Chadwick*

Above: Port Vale's Chris Neal makes a finger-tip save from Rory McArdle

Left: Gary Jones - Captain Fantastic - sounds the rallying call to the Valley Parade faithful

Below: The Management – Phil Parkinson and Steve Parkin

Gary Chadwick

Above: Rory McArdle wheels away after scoring against Aston Villa

Middle: City walk onto the Wembley pitch to a rapturous reception

Below: Nathan Doyle runs away from Michu as City make a first losing visit to Wembley in the Capital One final

Gintare Karpaviciute; Gary Chadwick

Capital performances: City celebrate after beating Aston Villa

Below: The inquest begins in the Villa defence as James Hanson celebrates his crucial second-leg goal

Gintare Karpaviciute

Above: Jon McLaughlin shows just what play-off success means to the Bantams

Gintare Karpaviciute

Above: Champagne flows in the City changing room after victory over Northampton

Right: Rory McArdle doubles City's lead in the play-off final

Below: James Hanson puts the Bantams ahead against the Cobblers

Above: The hard work is done - the party can begin

Below: City were welcomed back to Bradford by thousands of their fans

Bottom: The City Gents celebrate at Wembley

Gintare Karpaviciute

Heroes and Villains

"In professional sport, it is not uncommon for a side to pull off one giant-killing act in a season..."

Tickets for the Villa game had gone on sale soon after the win over Accrington

And on the first day alone, the club sold 9,000 for the home leg and over 2,500 for the return in Birmingham.

On the day of the game there would be 22,000-plus inside the ground and they, along with boss Phil Parkinson, sensed there might be an upset.

In professional sport it is not uncommon for a side to pull off one giant-killing act in a season.

Football history is littered with the likes of Hereford, Colchester and Wycombe, who have all over achieved once only to slip up next time out.

City had already claimed a couple of high-profile scalps and had beaten four higher division sides in their five games on their way to the semi-final.

Surely they would be unable to go to the well again?

In the build-up to the contest against a Villa side who, despite coming from behind to beat Ipswich the previous weekend, were badly out of sorts, Parkinson thought he had spotted a glimmer.

'We have to take advantage of the fact they've conceded a lot of goals,' he said.

'It doesn't matter what level you play at, if you concede that number of goals then there is a vulnerability there, confidence-wise.

'They'll look at Saturday's win as a big bonus, but prior to that they had let in a lot.'

And, like the fans on their way to Valley Parade, he was relishing yet another chance to pull off a shock.

'It will be exactly the same, it is a bonus for us to be playing these games,' he added.

'We didn't expect to win against Arsenal, but we did and now we get two more games against a Premier League side.

'I think it's great for our young players because it is an experience that will never leave them and will benefit them and us hugely.'

You knew it was a big game when World Cup final referee Howard Webb was announced as the official who would take charge of the first leg.

The four-letter surname also boded well after Roger East had been in charge for the tie at Wigan and Mike Dean had overseen the victory against Arsenal.

The game itself was a real nerve-jangler as Villa, despite their precarious league position, started confidently.

And Christian Benteke had more than enough heading chances to have ended the Bantams' hopes inside the opening stages.

Twice the Belgian was denied by Matt Duke, who had

another outstanding game, and twice he failed to hit the target when well placed.

But there was a real belief in the City ranks and they broke the deadlock after 19 minutes when Nahki Wells swept the ball home after a Zavon Hines effort had ricocheted into his path.

There was hesitation on the pitch and in the stands as everyone checked to make sure the linesman's flag stayed down.

When it did, the celebrations began.

Big James Hanson had a shot cleared off the line by Villa's former City youngster Fabian Delph, while the visitors went close through Benteke and Gabby Agbonlahor before the unthinkable happened: City bagged a second.

Gary Jones was the supplier of the cross from the left and Rory McArdle timed his run towards the near post perfectly, enabling him to head home.

City fans were in dreamland and it was almost 3-0 as a diving Hanson header thumped against the woodwork.

Thoughts of Wembley were put on hold when Andy Weimann sneaked in to pull one back for Paul Lambert's side with eight minutes remaining.

But Bradford were not knocked out of their stride and restored their two-goal advantage in the 88th minute with a goal straight out of Carl McHugh's childhood wish list.

Growing up in Donegal, the teenage defender idolised Republic of Ireland keeper Shay Given.

Now, in front of a packed house at Valley Parade and millions across the world on TV, he was heading powerfully past his childhood hero.

Could it get any better?

The final whistle was greeted in the stands with wild celebrations to match those after the Arsenal shoot-out.

But the players' reaction was more muted as they realised that, in line with the old football cliché, it was only half-time.

And there were no triumphant post match interviews or wild changing room celebrations.

While thrilled to have taken another massive scalp, Parkinson knew there was another tough challenge to come two weeks later.

He said: 'We're absolutely delighted with the way we played, obviously, because from the first minute to the last the lads were tremendous.

'But equally we know we're only halfway there, we've got a very difficult job in a fortnight's time.'

Parkinson added that his team had played better than in their stunning quarter-final win over the Gunners.

'Against Arsenal it was a great night for us, but I think the all-round performance tonight was better,' he said.

'Villa played a very attacking team and we had to defend well, and equally they left a lot of space on the pitch for us to play.

'Our quality players had to stay composed on the ball and they certainly did that.'

There were three games scheduled before the second leg, but Parkinson allowed himself a little peek into the future.

'We need to get a good start down there and get their fans on their backs,' he said.

'They'll have tremendous support and we have to do what we did here tonight, but better.

'The main thing is we can't go there and be complacent, because if we are then we will be punished. We haven't achieved anything yet.'

It seemed Parkinson was right to be cautious as Villa

boss Paul Lambert was still talking up his chances of going to Wembley.

'We're still in the tie, absolutely,' he said. 'It'll be a different game at home. It's only half-time.

'You have to regroup and go again. We've got to come out of the blocks. There's no grey area. We know what we have to do. We have to play better.'

Villa also had to defend set-pieces better as City were starting to make a habit of scoring important goals from corners and free-kicks.

Fans swamped the ticket office, quickly snapping up the remaining tickets for the second leg at Villa Park.

It would be another special night in a season of special nights for a team that was destined to make history.

League Cup - Semi-final - First Leg
January 8 - Aston Villa (H) W 3-1
City scorers: Wells 19; McArdle 77; McHugh 88
Duke, Darby, McHugh, McArdle, Good, Atkinson, Jones, Doyle, Hines (Turgott 65), Hanson, Wells. Unused substitutes: McLaughlin, Ravenhill, Reid, Jones, Hannah, Connell
Referee: Webb. Attendance: 22,245

On the ball: Kyel Reid takes on the Port Vale defence *Gary Chadwick*

A Winter's Tale

"It looked touch and go as to whether Phil Parkinson would leave Valley Parade..."

Before City could turn their attentions to a second game against Villa, the Bantams had six league points to play for, as well as a Johnstone's Paints Trophy trip to Crewe.

And they appeared to have a fight on their hands for boss Phil Parkinson, who was being heavily linked with the vacant manager's job at Championship side Blackpool.

At one stage it looked touch and go as to whether he would leave Valley Parade when the Tangerines were given permission to speak to him.

But he declined the opportunity to see what the west coast side had to offer, handing everyone at City a massive boost ahead of some important games.

First up was a home game with Oxford, a side they had beaten comfortably in September to go fourth in the League Two table.

City handed debuts to Andy Gray - for the second

time in his career - and Ryan Dickson, drafted in on loan from Southampton to try to fix the left back problem caused by James Meredith's debilitating bout of glandular fever.

And all was going well for the Bantams as Nahki Wells, capitalising on a catastrophic mix-up between centre back Michael Duberry and keeper Wayne Brown, fired them in front after just 14 minutes.

But Oxford levelled within four minutes as Sean Rigg blasted home from the edge of the area.

And, after Stephen Darby had been penalised for bringing down Alfie Potter, Peter Leven scored from the spot in the final minute to complete a comeback win.

United boss Chris Wilder admitted after that it had been the perfect time for his side to come to Valley Parade.

It was a third defeat in four league games and Parkinson suggested the exertions against Villa might have played their part.

'It was a bit flat, which maybe you'd expect after Tuesday,' he said. 'The ref gave a really poor decision with the penalty, but you get spoiled by having Howard Webb on Tuesday then the officials we had.'

League Two officials were something everyone would have to get used to again before the season ended.

But, in fairness to Parkinson, he did have a point.

City were, of course, still battling to get to Wembley on two fronts although, in contrast to most seasons, the JPT route was looking the less likely of the two.

A trip to League One Crewe Alexandra on a Tuesday night was hardly ideal and the fact the game had been delayed for a week was further evidence of a successful season on so many fronts.

Temperatures had plunged again and there was an element of doubt surrounding the game as players and fans started to arrive at the stadium. But no one in the City ranks wanted another postponement and, apparently, nor did the match officials who performed a cursory inspection by digging their heels into the turf close to the players' tunnel.

It is unclear how far in they managed to get them in, but it was sufficient for the game to go ahead.

The surface was changing colour in front of everyone's eyes, switching from the bright green it had been when the floodlights were switched on to a more frosted greeny-white.

As for the game, as expected Parkinson ignored the competition rules that state you must field six of the side that had played in the previous game by making eight changes - only Andy Gray, Ryan Dickson and Nathan Doyle survived from the Oxford defeat with most of those left out not even required to travel.

The 439 City fans in the Ice Cream Van Stand on the far side from the main stand for the northern semi-final at Gresty Road, soon had something to cheer as Kyel Reid let fly with a shot that went through the keeper's arms to put the Bantams ahead.

Byron Moore levelled for Alex on the stroke of half-time and three goals in the final 13 minutes, from Max Clayton, Brad Inman and Chuks Aneke, completed a 4-1 comeback.

It was a disappointment to lose - it was only City's second reverse in 13 cup ties - but probably more than welcome for a squad that was starting to show signs of wear around the edges.

Despite the defeat, which was nowhere near as heavy as the scoreline suggests, City were handed a boost post-match with the news they had secured the services of no nonsense centre-back Michael Nelson from SPL side

Kilmarnock - a player who had won the Scottish League Cup 12 months earlier in a shock win over Celtic.

Would that be an omen?

Given the latest bout of appalling weather there was already some conjecture that a second trip to the Potteries the following Saturday to face high flying Port Vale in the league would not take place.

And reports that the covers protecting the pitch had actually stuck to the surface only reinforced those views.

There was no let up in the days leading up to the game and it was no surprise when the plug was pulled 24 hours before the scheduled kick-off.

In the grand scheme of things, with the second leg at Villa Park looming large, it was not a major disappointment.

League Two

January 12 - Oxford United (H) L 1-2

City scorer: Wells 14

Duke, Darby, Dickson, McHugh, McArdle, Atkinson (Reid 63), G Jones, Doyle, Hines (Turgott 63), Gray, Wells (Connell 79). Unused substitutes: McLaughlin, Good, Ravenhill, R Jones, Turgott

Referee: Simpson. Attendance: 10,087

Football League Trophy - Northern Section - Semi-final

January 15 - Crewe (A) L 1-4

City scorer: Reid 18

McLaughlin, Dickson (McHugh 84), Naylor, Good, Ravenhill, Reid, R Jones, Doyle, Turgott, Gray (Hines 66), Connell (Wells 66). Unused substitutes: Duke, Brown

Referee: Miller. Attendance: 2,935

Aston Smartin'

"It is a magical day but this is what happens in cups, magic happens.."

Going to the Midlands, City were in the unenviable position of being favourites to reach Wembley.

That was not a major surprise, however, given they had a two-goal advantage as they travelled to Villa Park.

The City fans were certainly dreaming - 6,000 of them had managed to get tickets and they streamed south on a freezing night, the motorways edged with the snow that had been causing so many problems over the previous days.

The national Press's big hitters were out in force again. But the players had been sheltered in the build-up to the game, largely due to the weather.

The snow had been so bad around the City training ground and Valley Parade that the pre-match Press conference had been cancelled.

Few had been given the chance to speak to any of the management or playing squad before they set off.

A couple of media outlets did manage to snatch a word with Phil Parkinson moments before he met up with the rest of the travelling crew.

And, as his team set off to train at the Football Association centre of excellence at St George's Park in Burton, he was in no doubt what his team had to do in the second leg - attack.

'Aston Villa carry a real threat going forward but their weakness is defensively,' he said. 'It would be foolish for us to go there to defend for 90 minutes.

'We have to carry a threat ourselves and we certainly will. The best way for us to progress is to score and we will endeavour to do that. I've used the word desire a lot this season and we have got that in abundance.

'One thing for the game is that if things go against us at any stage we won't give in, and if players are tiring then we'll have three subs who will come on and give us every chance.'

Telling the players to attack and then actually carrying out the instructions would be two entirely different things.

The Villa Park pitch was, as you would expect, perfect. And the vastness of the famous old stadium which had staged so many big games almost took the breath away.

By kick-off there would be 40,000 inside with the vast majority hoping against hope that the Premier League strugglers would be able to restore the natural order and take their place in the final.

How would the City players react? One thing they had to do was keep it tight for as long as possible.

The Villa hierarchy had decided that they needed to generate some atmosphere and had placed a flag in the team's colours on every home fan's seat.

They were waved furiously by 34,000 people as the players entered the arena, but it all seemed exactly what it was - a bit false.

Perhaps the City players could sense that as they set about their business, although the home side, as you would have expected, had the better of the opening exchanges.

Matt Duke made a couple of big saves as City maintained their advantage and passed the midway point of the first half. Then Villa struck.

Christian Benteke, who looked so poor in the air over both legs, stole in at the near post to fire home a Joe Bennett cross. It was going to be a real test for the Bantams now and there were some anxious moments as Charles N'Zogbia and Stephen Ireland forced Duke to save again.

City's only effort on goal came from Nahki Wells who curled the ball wide from the edge of the area.

It was a nervous West Yorkshire contingent in the Press room at half-time with Villa needing to score just one more to force extra-time. A Bradford goal would change all that and ten minutes into the second half the dream was well and truly alive again.

City had prospered from set-pieces on three occasions in the first leg, so when they won a 55th-minute corner, 6,000 travelling fans in the North Stand were on their feet.

Skipper Gary Jones delivered and James Hanson powered his header past Shay Given and into the back of the net. Cue delirium in the away end and the iconic moment of the cup run from BBC Leeds summariser Wayne Jacobs.

He had always been calm, even at the break when the tie could have gone either way. As the ball crossed the Villa goalline, he was ready to react.

'Cometh the hour, cometh the Big Man,' he bellowed.

Hanson, a supermarket shelf stacker in his non-

League days with Guiseley, had written his name into Bradford City folklore.

There was still work to do, of course.

It would have been a far more comfortable evening all round had a thunderous shot from Garry Thompson not bounced back off the bar with 18 minutes of the game remaining. And there were a few late nerves when Andreas Weimann scored Villa's second in the 89th minute.

But nothing was going to stop history being made and City saw out four minutes of added-time to book their place in the final.

Phil Dowd's whistle signalled wild celebrations on the pitch, although the enormity of taking a third top-flight scalp surely could not so easily be summed up.

The players did their best to put their achievements into words.

'This is dreamland, hopefully we will have a great following at Wembley and do the club proud,' said keeper Matt Duke. 'I am not convinced it will ever sink in.

'You dream of this as a kid, playing at Wembley, and I just want to do the club proud.'

As he had been after the win over Arsenal, veteran skipper Gary Jones said he was lost for words.

He managed to find a few, though: 'To come here and get the result we have is amazing, we played really well. It is a magical day but that is what happens in cups, magic happens. We knew would be on the back foot from the word go, but we have some resilience and spirit and it was a fantastic goal from James Hanson.'

City would have to wait to find out their final opponents - Swansea City would close out their semi-final against Chelsea 24 hours later - but co-chairman Mark Lawn was already dreaming of winning at the National Stadium.

'If we get into Europe I'll have to start learning some languages!' he said. 'I don't care who we get in the final, they will probably both batter us. Chelsea will have to declare at half-time if we play them!'

Boss Phil Parkinson was in no doubt about the magnitude of the team's achievements in just getting through to the final. 'These lads will be remembered in the history of Bradford City for years to come,' he said.

'There's a 1911 lounge at the club to celebrate the cup victory of that year. Well, in years to come, there will be a lounge named after this cup run and these players because of what they've achieved.

'To go to Wembley is going to keep the club going for quite a while, I imagine.

'For the city of Bradford, it's massive and I really feel that this can galvanise the area.'

There was a month of league football between the semi-final and the final and City could not afford to lose ground on the teams occupying the promotion places.

An appearance at Wembley in a major cup final would be the highlight of many a player's career.

But Parkinson believed there and then that his squad had enough to combine their incredible cup exploits with a tilt at promotion to League One.

'The cup is probably bigger now because we're in the final, but we're greedy and we want both,' he said.

'We've found it difficult to get going after some of our cup games and that is understandable.

'Having said that, I think we're good enough to get our league campaign back on track and look forward to our Wembley game.'

Did he believe that or did he have to say it?

Either way, his words would be prophetic.

League Two		31 January 2013		
		P	GD	Pts
1	Gillingham	28	24	55
2	Port Vale	28	26	53
3	Burton Albion	30	1	46
4	Northampton	29	7	45
5	Exeter	29	3	45
6	Cheltenham	28	3	45
7	Southend	28	13	43
8	Fleetwood	28	9	43
9	Rotherham	27	3	43
10	**Bradford**	27	5	40
11	Chesterfield	29	5	39
12	Oxford Utd	28	-2	39
13	Torquay	27	2	37
14	Rochdale	29	-1	37
15	Dag & Red	30	-1	37
16	York	29	-2	37
17	Morecambe	29	-2	36
18	Wycombe	28	-7	36
19	Accrington	29	-15	31
20	Barnet	29	-13	29
21	Aldershot	28	-14	29
22	Plymouth	29	-10	28
23	Bristol Rovers	27	-16	28
24	Wimbledon	27	-18	27

League Cup - Semi-final - Second Leg
January 22 - Aston Villa (A) L 1-2 (*won 4-3 on aggregate*)
City scorer: Hanson 55
Duke, Darby, McHugh, McArdle, Good, Hines (Thompson 71), Jones, Doyle, Atkinson, Hanson, Wells (Turgott 87).
Unused substitutes: McLaughlin, Ravenhill, Reid, Connell, Nelson.
Referee: Dowd. Attendance: 40,193

Cup Distraction?

"The weather relented and City continued to play catch-up on the teams above them.."

Phil Parkinson was right about his side finding it difficult after cup ties.

In nine league games played after a knock-out clash, City had managed just a couple of wins, and they had lost six times.

Next up were Wycombe at Valley Parade, although the continuing bad weather would account for that game.

And the club took the opportunity of a rare midweek break to jet the squad off to Tenerife for some warm weather training.

On their return they would be heading to a far less grand seaside destination - Fleetwood.

But with both sides battling for the play-offs as a minimum, it was another big game for the Bantams.

Alan Goodall put the home side ahead midway through the first half, but City were level before the break,

Nahki Wells firing a 25-yard free-kick in for his 18th goal of the season.

Southampton loanee left back Ryan Dickson bagged his first-ever goal for City seven minutes after the restart.

But Fleetwood secured a share of the spoils with 15 minutes remaining when cup hero James Hanson was judged to have handled in the area and Jon Parkin's spot-kick somehow managed to wriggle under Matt Duke's body.

Dropping three points was disappointing; seeing defender Rory McArdle leave Highbury Stadium on crutches with a protective boot on a damaged ankle was alarming.

With 22 days to a major cup final he and the City fans had their fingers crossed that it was not going to be a major problem.

Given that he had only missed the Johnstone Paints Trophy games against Port Vale and Crewe because he was rested and the League clash with York because he was in Portugal with Northern Ireland he would leave a big hole.

With Andrew Davies still struggling with the injury he picked up at Burton in October, much was going to rest on Michael Nelson, who made his debut at Fleetwood.

And he was in the side again when City returned to Valley Parade for the first time since their win at Villa to face the division leaders Gillingham.

City had slipped to tenth in the table after the draw at Fleetwood, their lowest placing since early September.

And they dropped a further two places as the table-topping Gills claimed their tenth away win of the campaign thanks to Cody McDonald's second-half strike.

City had been the better side for long spells, but were unable to find a way through - a familiar story during the run - and the defeat meant they had taken just two points from the 15 on offer since the Boxing Day win over Accrington Stanley. It was not the kind of form that boded particularly well for a re-arranged midweek trip to a Wycombe side that was on a three-match winning run.

But that is what faced City as the weather relented for the time being and they continued to play catch-up on the teams above them.

Wycombe share their Adams Park home with Aviva Premiership rugby union side London Wasps and, despite the undersoil heating to help the groundstaff, you could tell by the look of the pitch.

It was a mess and the immediate worry was that it might not suit City's style of play.

Much of the talk before kick-off was about the lack of goals from midfield.

But that was soon put to bed as Nathan Doyle slammed home the opening goal inside 55 seconds.

It was the start the Bantams craved and it laid the platform for a much-needed win.

After Garry Thompson had hit the woodwork, Will Atkinson doubled their lead with nine minutes remaining.

And Doyle bagged his second of the game - and the season - from the penalty spot two minutes later, after substitute James Hanson had been brought down in the area.

It was a crucial win for Phil Parkinson's side, who were still five points outside the play-offs albeit with a game in hand on most of the sides at the top.

It also meant the trip to the Cherry Red Records Stadium for a game against Wimbledon was crucial.

Three points against a side battling to beat the return to the Conference would be just the boost the Bantams needed eight days before their date with Swansea.

Key figure: Captain Gary Jones led City to the Capital One Cup final *Gintare Karpaviciute*

And when Garry Thompson volleyed them in front around the hour mark all was well.

A bobbly pitch prevented Thompson from doubling the visitors' lead and they paid a heavy price as, having dominated for 83 minutes, Jack Midson and Gary Alexander bagged the goals that gave the Dons the points.

Parkinson appeared as stunned as the fans who had packed into the compact ground.

'I can't believe we have lost the game,' he said. 'I can't believe we haven't won it, never mind drawn it.

'We have dominated the game, but obviously couldn't get the second goal.

'The dressing room was a very quiet place. I couldn't really have faulted the way we played and to come away with nothing is really hard to take.

'This defeat is hurting because it was an unjust one.'

It was a disappointing trip to the capital and not the way City would have wanted to have warmed up for their historic appearance in the Capital One Cup final.

League Two
February 2 - Fleetwood (A) D 2-2
City scorers: Wells 44; Dickson 52
Duke, Darby, McArdle (Dickson 41), Nelson, McHugh, Thompson (Reid 80), Jones, Doyle, Atkinson, Hanson, Wells (Gray 85). Unused substitutes: McLaughlin, Ravenhill, Connell, Hines.
Referee: Robinson. Attendance: 3,577

League Two
February 9 - Gillingham (H) L 0-1
Duke, Darby, Naylor (Connell 81), Nelson, Good (Thompson 73), Hines (Dickson 73), Doyle, Jones, Reid, Hanson, Wells. Unused substitutes: McLaughlin, Davies, Gray, Atkinson.
Referee: Boyeson. Attendance: 10,087

League Two
February 12 - Wycombe (A) W 3-0
City scorers: Doyle 1, 83; Atkinson 81
Duke, Darby, Dickson, Nelson, Davies (McHugh 87), Jones, Doyle, Atkinson, Reid, Thompson, Gray (Hanson 72).
Unused substitutes: McLaughlin, Connell, Wells, Turgott, Good
Referee: Mathieson. Attendance: 3,068

League Two
February 16 - AFC Wimbledon (A) L 1-2
City scorer: Thompson 59
Duke; Darby, Dickson, Nelson, Davies; Jones, Doyle, Atkinson, Reid (Wells 85); Thompson, Gray (Hanson 65).
Unused substitutes: McLaughlin, McHugh, Hines, Turgott, Good,
Referee: Bratt. Attendance: 4,320

Wembley: Part One

"Four goals down and with 20 minutes still remaining, 34,000 fans got to their feet.."

City's appearance in the Capital One Cup had been hanging over the club from the moment the final whistle went in the semi-final second leg at Villa Park.

The smell of the new cloth from the players' Wembley suits and leather from their shiny new shoes that were delivered more than a fortnight before the big game brought it closer.

And the proliferation of Cup final songs - the pick of which was 'Let's Get Ready for Wembley' released by the Bantams Banter boys and including the timeless Wembley/trembly rhyme - meant the official build-up had begun.

There was also the blessing from City's biggest 'celebrity' fan, the Dalai Lama, whose picture holding his number 14 shirt was becoming very familiar.

And fans snapped up tickets in their thousands -

21,000 went on the first day they were available - and a little more than 2,000 of the initial allocation left for general sale after season ticket and flexi card holders had got hold of theirs.

The queues snaked round Valley Parade, with some supporters camping overnight in freezing temperatures to guarantee they would not be disappointed.

But the enormity of what was about to happen to the club really dawned on the Tuesday before the game when Valley Parade was buzzing with media types for the official club cup final news conference.

More than an hour before the official start time, television crews from France, Norway and Japan were filming the stadium from every conceivable angle.

Waiting for the players and management to arrive in the Stuart McCall and John Hendrie Suites at Valley Parade, journalists were even reduced to interviewing each other.

Opportunistic vendors sold half-and-half scarves and flags on Manningham Lane, and there was another cup final song being touted by a Manchester-based singer.

It was some distance from a normal pre-match conference attended by four or five locals at most.

There were some similarities; the hospitality stretched to no more than a cup of tea or coffee.

And the players and management were open to all manner of questions, more than willing to give up their time.

As one writer quipped, had this been a top Premier League side you would have been lucky to get one player let alone a dozen or more.

All the national newspapers were represented and they were filled in with background information on the members of the squad who, for a few days at least, would become household names.

Much of the focus surrounded star player Nahki Wells, cup run hero Matt Duke and former shop worker James Hanson - the only player in the squad that had reached Wembley to actually cost City a transfer fee.

Wells had always been big news in his Bermudian homeland, a national hero even, but this had gone off the scale.

Duke had won his battle with testicular cancer to continue his career.

And Hanson had been plucked from non League Guiseley, where he combined his football with shelf stacking duties at the Co-op.

Everywhere you looked there was a story.

Duke, a man with seemingly limitless patience in front of the media throughout the cup run, had been an unused substitute for Hull City at Wembley in the Championship play-off, while Wells and Hanson were making their first ever visit to the national stadium.

At the other end of the scale, Garry Thompson was about to appear at the most famous stadium in the world for a remarkable fourth time.

He scored for Morecambe in their Conference play-off final against Exeter City in 2007 and was part of the Scunthorpe squad that made two appearances there in 2008-2009, tasting defeat in the Johnstone's Paint Trophy final against Luton Town, before winning promotion to the Championship by defeating Millwall 3-2.

'It will be amazing,' he told the assembled media. 'We just need to make sure nerves don't get the better of us and we go out there and play our football and stay in the game as long as possible.

'There's no reason why we can't go there and win.

'Swansea are an excellent passing side. I think they've

been compared to Arsenal and obviously having watched *Match of the Day* and you see some of the goals they score, they are a good footballing team. But it's 11 men versus 11 men and that's how we look at it.'

Interest in Donegal was high with centre-back Carl McHugh revealing 111 friends and family - a fitting number as the man he would replace against Swansea was called Nelson - would be inside the stadium on cup final day.

It was going to be a big day for a player given an opportunity on the pre-season tour of his home country having been released by Reading.

'It's a big number, but it's not just family,' said McHugh. 'My mum and dad have sorted it all out and people have just given the money to them, so at least I haven't had to pay for them.

'That would be about a year's wages for me!

'The majority are from Donegal, plus a few others who I've played football with down the years.'

The man most in demand on press day was, understandably, manager Phil Parkinson who had masterminded the incredible cup run.

He had spent the entire season banging the drum for promotion to League One.

But as the big day in the capital approached, his focus changed.

'All along the league has been our priority,' he said. 'I cannot hide away from that.

'But we are in the final at Wembley and have a chance of getting into Europe.

'So I can honestly say now, if we had the choice of two things, it would have to be winning the cup.

'We are a League Two team. We have created history by getting this far.

'It would be truly amazing if we could pull it off.'

As the dust settled and the scribes went away to write their previews, the enormity of City's task began to hit home.

And a couple of days later the players got another taste of the cup fever that enveloped the club as they gathered for their journey south.

The team normally leaves for an away trip with minimal fuss. On this occasion fans gathered to wave off their hopes who were interviewed in front of the TV cameras as they boarded the coach.

As was to be expected, the *Telegraph & Argus* offered wall-to-wall coverage of the big event.

And their mammoth Cup Final Special has to have been unique: it had not one single piece with a current player, football writer Simon Parker working overtime to cover the event from every possible angle.

The build-up on local TV and radio was a step up for the norm as well.

There were three hour-long specials on BBC Radio Leeds, while the TV had a half hour on the impact of the final on the city as a whole.

And the send-off was marked by a live broadcast from the stadium on Friday night.

This was clearly no ordinary game.

On a normal match weekend travelling the length and breadth of the country, you might pass - or more likely be passed by - a handful of cars carrying City fans.

They'd had an impressive away support from the first day of the season, but travelling down the M1 from West Yorkshire you could not help but be struck by the number of flags, scarves and car stickers in claret and amber.

And this was on the Saturday, more than 24 hours before the game.

London was awash with fans, the majority from West Yorkshire, many from elsewhere and a good number from overseas.

Saturday night was party night, whether it was in the centre of the capital or in the sprawling suburbs.

Hotels were full of fans and the great thing was that Bradford fans mingled with their Swansea counterparts without a hint of a problem.

Some of the conversations were revealing.

One group were discussing the merits of Bradford's keepers matt Duke and Jon McLaughlin.

'Will Duke play?' asked one, of the stopper who had made the position his own.

'Think so. The other one's good as well, though.'

'What's his name?'

You got the feeling that a regular at Valley Parade would have known the name of 'the other one'.

With kick-off at 4pm, there seemed little likelihood of there being too many people on Olympic Way by 10.30, when the various broadcasters were planning to assemble.

How wrong could we all have been?

Stepping off the tube at Wembley Park really got the adrenaline going.

And the fact that there was already an abundance of claret and amber on show only heightened the excitement.

Say what you like about Wembley, the venue is right up there with the best in the world.

And even the underpasses dripped with a sense of occasion, posters chronicling the paths both Bradford and Swansea had taken to the final.

The lampposts were adorned in both clubs' colours and every poster was a quiz question about games from previous rounds.

It was truly a special day.

The BBC bus was parked in the shadow of the stadium, housing not only BBC Leeds, but both BBC Wales and BBC Cymru, as well as BBC 5Live.

It was a magnet for fans, many in fancy dress, of both teams and they were all determined to enjoy the biggest day of their clubs' histories.

It would have been rude not to have taken a walk up to the Bobby Moore statue outside Wembley's front door.

The flags were at half mast to commemorate the 20th anniversary of his death.

Looking at the only man to have skippered England to World Cup glory you could not help but think how a man who led second division Fulham in an FA Cup final late in his career would have approved of two of footballs smaller clubs enjoying their day in the sun.

As the early arrivers wandered round the outside of the stadium, stewards were assembling ready for their day's work.

There were more stewards waiting for their instructions than there had been spectators inside the Cherry Red Records Stadium eight days earlier.

Back at the BBC bus, the sun was shining as the crowds increased in size by the minute, but the wind was biting and, unusually for a big showpiece occasion, there was the hint of snow in the air.

Ironically, that might have added to the pre-match spectacle as most were wrapped in their club's colours.

Once inside the ground, the enormity of the occasion began to hit home.

This was Wembley.

There were 80,000 empty red seats surrounding a bowling green of a playing surface.

A giant replica of the famous three-handled League Cup was being built on the far side of the pitch and there was an enormous football in one corner.

There was even a buzz in the Press room with few watching the game between Manchester City and Chelsea on the big screens.

Interestingly, word spread that the Bradford players would not be doing a Wembley walk.

They had been to the stadium the night before to have a look round and it was felt that an appearance on the pitch before they came out to warm up would be too mentally fatiguing.

Swansea's squad did appear in their finery although there were far more Bradford fans than Swansea followers in their places when they emerged from the tunnel.

The roar when the two teams walked out for kick-off was bigger than any of the Bradford fans could have imagined.

Flags placed on each seat inside the vast arena were waved furiously.

But one big flag caught the attention of most.

It was the flag to remember the 56 who perished in the Valley Parade fire and it was carried over the heads of the City fans as they waited for their modern day heroes to emerge.

And there was a real mixture of excitement and nervousness as the game finally got underway

As a football match, things could hardly have gone much worse for Bradford.

Having weathered the early storm, Parkinson's side ventured forward tentatively, lost the ball and conceded the first goal.

The manager must have been desperate to get his side

in at the break without further setbacks, but Swansea doubled their advantage five minutes before half-time.

And, with a solid start to the second half a prerequisite, Bradford found themselves three goals behind within two minutes of the restart.

As a contest - and it hadn't been much of one in the opening 45 minutes - it was well and truly over.

Just when no one thought things could get any worse, Matt Duke was shown a red card and Swansea scored their fourth from the penalty spot.

And the footballing lesson was completed by a fifth in injury-time.

By that time, the Bradford faithful were resigned to their fate and their reaction was quite remarkable.

Four goals down and with 20 minutes still remaining, 34,000 fans got to their feet and waved their flags.

It was the most amazing sight ever seen at the National stadium.

Unlike the pre-planned efforts of Aston Villa in the semi final when the Premier League club tried to create a positive atmosphere, this sent a tingle down the spine and provided an uplifting distraction from what was unfolding on the pitch.

Swansea's fans joined in sporadically, but it was if they were happy for Bradford to bask in the glory of what had been a remarkable journey.

City won a late corner, which was greeted with the biggest roar of the game and when Gary Jones dragged a tame shot wide of goal it was as if they had bagged a last gasp winner.

Boss Parkinson was left to reflect on an historic afternoon that had, in all honesty, failed to live up to the pre-final hype.

'Obviously, for our supporters and everybody we would've loved to have made more of a game of it, but it was a tough afternoon,' Parkinson told reporters.

'We conceded after 16 minutes against a very good side and when it nearly gets to half-time at 1-0 down we try to change things around [and leak another goal].

'We did make a few adjustments after the break and one of them was to get up the pitch another 15-20 yards because we were playing too deep, but we conceded straight after the break as well.

'And then, lo and behold, our goalie gets sent off after 60 minutes, which is a decision I felt the ref could have used his common sense for in terms of the context of the game.

'We were 3-0 down against a Premiership team and there's a penalty awarded against us. With the greatest respect, I don't think at that stage we were going to come back to win 5-4, so I think he could've used a bit of discretion and given Matt a yellow card.'

Parkinson added that nothing in Swansea's impressive display had surprised him or his players

'Swansea are a very, very good team,' he said. 'We had them watched and spoke to a lot of Premier League managers about them and everyone kept coming back to me saying "...there's not many weaknesses in this team."

'They are a very good side and they showed it. They have a team that has a good balance because they keep the ball and have forwards that make great runs behind your back four as well. So they have a lot of threats and clever players with pace and just the general all round movement was difficult for us to cope with.

'And on that big Wembley pitch against so many good players it was tough.'

Despite coming out on the wrong end of the worst

defeat in a League Cup final, Parkinson said his players have much to be proud of.

'They [the players] were a bit down in the dressing room because we could've played better and we are a better team than we probably showed,' he said. 'But equally I told the lads to get their heads up because what you have achieved is outstanding.

'The lads have been magnificent the way they have conducted themselves throughout this extra exposure, which is unprecedented for a team at our level. The way they have conducted themselves has been outstanding.'

Parkinson praised Bradford's supporters who stood by their team when the chips were down.

'The highlight for the day for me was the way the supporters stayed behind the team throughout the game,' he said.

'I think everybody realised what an enormous achievement this has been from a club from the fourth tier of English football to get to a major final.

'Of course I would've loved to be sat here talking about a great performance and a great game. But what Swansea did to us today they've done to Premier League teams. They are an outstanding side and enormous credit to the job Michael Laudrup has done.'

Swansea had formed a guard of honour for the City players as they went up to collect their runners-up medals - losers medals would surely not detract from everything that had gone before the final.

Then there was an explosion of noise - mostly from the pyrotechnics - as the Swans were handed the three-handled trophy.

The Wembley turf was strewn with tickertape and the fans began to ponder the journey home.

Once the dust had settled on the game and performances had been pored over by the Press box 'experts', the clean up started.

And it provided one of the more surreal moments of the whole day as an army of groundstaff moved, inch by inch, across the pitch to clear the two-inch-long pieces of paper that had been propelled into the night sky by a couple of giant canons.

League Cup Final
February 24 - Swansea (Wembley) L 0-5
Duke, Darby, McHugh, McArdle, Good (Davies 46), Atkinson, Jones, Doyle, Thompson (Hines 73), Wells (McLaughlin 57), Hanson. Unused substitutes: Ravenhill, Reid, Connell, Turgott.
Referee: Friend. Attendance: 82,997

After the Lord Mayor's Show

"City entered the arena through a guard of honour and the fans waved their Wembley flags.."

It is not that far as the crow flies from Wembley to Dagenham - in footballing terms it is a million miles.

But it was Dagenham & Redbridge who offered City their next big test just three days later and the question everyone wanted answering was: How would the players - and the fans for that matter - cope?

Speaking to a group of supporters outside Valley Parade ahead of the game against the Daggers, I was surprised to hear they were pessimistic about the club's promotion chances.

To a man they were thrilled to have been part of the Wembley crowd, even if one had got fed up waving his flag by the end of the game.

But they were disappointed by what they felt was their team's failure to have a go against their fourth top-flight opponents of the run.

One said he was disappointed by City's style of play which he felt was too direct.

And they all wanted a creative midfielder with a goal-scoring striker also on their wish list.

But everyone I spoke to said that despite any reservations they might have had they would be backing the Bantams, no matter how the campaign panned out over the remaining 15 regular-season games.

We were about to see.

The City team entered the arena through a Dagenham & Redbridge guard of honour and the fans waved their Wembley flags.

But the game was a disappointment with James Hanson having to find an 86th-minute equaliser to claim a share of the spoils against a side whose long-term manager John Still had left for Conference outfit Luton 24 hours before kick-off.

For the moment, the result left City ten points behind seventh-placed Cheltenham with three games in hand, but they did at least show that the fighting spirit that had been evident all season was still there despite their Wembley experience.

'It could turn out to be a very good point because it was starting to look a bit desperate,' admitted assistant manager Steve Parkin.

'We had a big setback on Sunday [against Swansea] because we felt we let ourselves down. It was important we followed it up with a performance today.'

Big match nerves: City came back to earth with a bump in February *Gintare Karpaviciute*

League Two

February 27 - Dagenham & Redbridge (H) D 1-1

City scorer: Hanson 86

McLaughlin, Darby (Connell 78), Davies, Nelson, McArdle, Reid, Thompson (Wells 66), Jones, Doyle, Gray (Hanson 66), Hines. Unused substitutes: Bentley, McHugh, Ravenhill, Atkinson.

Referee: Sarginson. Attendance: 10,006

League Two				28 February 2013
		P	*GD*	*Pts*
1	Gillingham	34	25	65
2	Port Vale	34	30	63
3	Burton Albion	35	10	59
4	Northampton	35	10	58
5	Rotherham	33	7	56
6	Exeter	34	8	55
7	Cheltenham	35	4	55
8	Fleetwood	34	5	51
9	Southend	34	11	50
10	Morecambe	35	-1	46
11	Oxford Utd	34	-4	46
12	Wycombe	34	-6	45
13	**Bradford**	31	6	44
14	Chesterfield	34	5	44
15	Rochdale	34	-5	42
16	Dag & Red	34	-2	41
17	York	35	-10	40
18	Bristol Rovers	34	-14	39
19	Aldershot	35	-13	38
20	Torquay	34	-6	37
21	Barnet	34	-11	37
22	Accrington	34	-17	36
23	Wimbledon	34	-21	36
24	Plymouth	34	-11	33

The Longest March

"At that stage, there can't have been a single City fan who thought City would make the top seven..."

The nature of the campaign meant that there was little time to dwell on the game against the Daggers with trips to Yorkshire neighbours York City - game 48 in all competitions - and high flying Port Vale in four days.

York were in such appalling form - ten games without a win going onto the clash - that it was an away banker.

Of course, Bantams fans who had seen things go so spectacularly wrong over recent seasons saw potential banana skin as well. But they still turned out in numbers, selling out the away end on a glorious afternoon.

And their faith was rewarded as a decent away display culminated in late goals from James Hanson and Garry Thompson securing the points that kept the dream alive.

It also signalled the end for York manager Gary Mills who was sacked hours after the final whistle.

That was no concern of Bradford's, who turned their thoughts to Vale Park and a game against one of the two sides that had blazed a trail at the top of the table pretty much since day one.

City had won a Johnstone's Paint Trophy tie at the same ground before Christmas, but it was a very different Bradford side for the league game against a Vale team that included prolific striker Tom Pope.

And Jon McLaughlin had to be at his best to deny Pope on a couple of occasions in a pulsating game.

It ended goalless, but both sides had their chances, James Hanson having a header tipped onto the bar by Vale keeper Chris Neal early in the second half, while a Rory McArdle effort was cleared off the line.

Vale's Doug Loft was red-carded for a challenge on Ricky Ravenhill in injury-time and the teams ended with a point each. The Bantams remained nine points from the dotted line.

But a couple of games against struggling sides Aldershot and Plymouth, followed by a trip to play-off rivals Exeter, would surely see a step up in the challenge to force their way into the end-of-season party?

How wrong that proved to be.

Aldershot arrived in West Yorkshire perilously close to the League Two drop zone having jettisoned manager Dean Holdsworth less than a month before.

But they proved a resilient bunch as City dominated, firing in 14 shots to three and forcing 13 corners with the Shots unable to win even one.

They did get a free-kick in a dangerous position on the stroke of half time and went ahead as Kieron Cadogan found the back of the net from 25 yards.

City kept going, and going, and going.

And they eventually got their reward when Terrell Forbes fouled Zavon Hines in the eighth added minute and Alan Connell kept his cool to rescue a 1-1 draw.

It meant Phil Parkinson's side were still nine points behind with 11 games remaining and they had the chance to catch up with a trip to Devon to face a Plymouth side that went into the game at the foot of the table.

Around 250 City fans took a day off work to make the longest trip of the season but, in the end, the highlight of the game was the pre-match pasty.

There were chances over the 90 minutes but it was, in general, a poor Tuesday night for City.

Garry Thompson, who rattled the crossbar yet again, Kyel Reid and James Hanson went close, but at the other end Carl McHugh and Stephen Darby were both forced to clear off the line as the game ended goalless.

City remained nine points behind Exeter - the team in seventh - but with two games in hand, and the sides were set to meet four days later in a game that would give the Bantams the chance to close the gap to a more manageable proportion.

Perhaps strangely, City's players returned to West Yorkshire in between their two games in Devon.

And the second game could hardly have started any worse with a Craig Woodman corner hitting the post and going in off keeper Matt Duke's back after 11 minutes.

Things deteriorated further before the break when the impressive Lawson D'Ath made it 2-0 on the stroke of half-time.

Bradford cut the deficit when substitute Kyel Reid curled a 79th-minute corner into the net, but thoughts of a fightback were short lived as Scot Bennett blasted home from 20 yards five minutes later.

City, committing more and more players forward, were caught again as John O'Flynn bagged the Grecians' fourth to complete a miserable afternoon.

The Bantams were now 12 points adrift of Exeter with two games in hand and ten behind Rotherham, now in seventh, having played one game fewer.

Boss Phil Parkinson had continued his policy of rotating the squad for the game - a policy surely based on the mental and physical exertions his side had face against Swansea.

But he remained defiant, despite the odds now being firmly against his side reaching the play-offs.

'Whatever happens we have to make sure we finish the season in good spirits,' he said. 'After the season we have had we can't just let it peter out to nothing.

'I need to make sure I pick a team of players who understand that and are going to really have a go for us because I can't let the season drift into obscurity.'

They were the right words, but surely the promotion dream was finally over?

It emerged that the City players, having travelled back from St James' Park straight after the game, were in Bradford for a heart-to-heart meeting within 24 hours of the defeat.

It was by all accounts a 'home truths' affair, but history would show that it was the turning point in a campaign that threatened to meander towards mid-table.

The initial tangible result of the meeting was a first home league win of 2013, as a Garry Thompson goal after seven minutes proved enough to see off Wycombe on Tuesday 19 March, effectively ending the visitors' hopes of gatecrashing the play-offs themselves.

City were still seven points adrift, but the gap was

down to single figures and, in a way, seemed more achieveable with eight games to go.

It was still a long shot, but hopes were high as City prepared for the Good Friday visit of Southend United to Valley Parade.

The Shrimps had been City's opponents in the game that followed the Arsenal victory.

On that day, Bradford had appeared to be cruising to a maximum haul after leading 2-0 with ten minutes left.

Southend scored twice to level and start a league rot that produced just four wins in 16 games, a spell in which the team slid from fourth to 12th.

For this final game in a frustrating month for City, Phil Brown had taken over as Southend boss from Paul Sturrock and was taking charge of his first game.

His pre-match appearance on the pitch caused quite a stir; the sharp suit, unbuttoned white shirt and Tango suntan feeling very out of place at League Two level.

But his side continued the game where they had left off in December, with two goals in the opening 11 minutes.

At that stage there cannot have been a single City fan, no matter how die hard, who thought the Bantams could make it into the top seven come the end of the season.

Zavon Hines, who admitted after the game he had been among the poorer City players in the first half, reduced the arrears with a neat low finish eight minutes after the break.

And James Hanson ended a run of five games without a goal to give Phil Parkinson's side hope when he headed home a Nahki Wells cross with seven minutes remaining.

A mirror image of the first meeting between the sides had yielded another point.

But would it be enough?

League Two

March 2 - York City (A) W 2-0

City scorers: Hanson 77; Thompson 86

McLaughlin, Darby, Nelson, Davies, McHugh, Atkinson (Hines 67), Jones, Ravenhill, Reid, Wells (Thompson 55), Hanson. Unused substitutes: Gray, Duke, Connell, McArdle, Doyle.

Referee: D'Urso. Attendance: 5,678

League Two

March 5 - Port Vale (A) D 0-0

McLaughlin, Darby, McHugh, Nelson, McArdle, Jones (Doyle 90), Ravenhill, Atkinson, Hines (Reid 75), Hanson, Thompson (Wells 65). Unused substitutes: Duke, Davies, Gray, Connell.

Referee: Adcock. Attendance: 4,281

League Two

March 9 - Aldershot (H) D 1-1

City scorer: Connell 90 (pen)

McLaughlin, Darby, McHugh, Nelson (Connell 78), McArdle, Ravenhill (Reid 61), Atkinson, Jones, Hines, Hanson, Wells (Thompson 61). Unused substitutes: Duke, Davies, Doyle, Gray

Referee; Clark. Attendance: 10,397

League Two
March 12 - Plymouth Argyle (A) D 0-0
Duke, Darby, McArdle, Davies, McHugh, Hines (Atkinson 77), Doyle, Ravenhill, Reid, Thompson (Connell 80), Gray (Hanson 66). Unused substitutes: McLaughlin, Jones, Wells, Nelson.
Referee: Davies. Attendance: 5,609

League Two
March 16 - Exeter City (A) L 1-4
City scorer: Reid 79
Duke, Darby, McHugh, Davies, Nelson (Wells 83), Atkinson, Jones, Doyle (Hines 46), Connell, Thompson (Reid 46), Hanson. Unused substitutes: McLaughlin, Meredith, McArdle, Ravenhill
Referee: Salisbury. Attendance: 4,199

League Two
March 19 - Wycombe (H) W 1-0
City scorer: Thompson 7
McLaughlin; Darby, Davies, McArdle, Meredith; Hines (Atkinson 73), Jones, Ravenhill (Doyle 73), Reid; Hanson, Thompson (Wells 87). Unused substitutes: Duke, McHugh, Connell, Nelson.
Referee: Ilderton. Attendance: 8,047

League Two
March 29 - Southend United (H) D 2-2
City scorers: Hines 53; Hanson 83
McLaughlin, Darby (Wells 81), Meredith, Davies, McArdle, Ravenhill (Atkinson 73), Reid, Thompson, Jones, Hanson, Hines (Connell 73). Unused substitutes: Duke, McHugh, Nelson, Doyle
Referee: Rushton. Attendance: 10,598

League Two				31 March 2013
		P	*GD*	*Pts*
1	Gillingham	40	27	75
2	Port Vale	40	29	70
3	Northampton	40	11	68
4	Burton Albion	39	10	66
5	Cheltenham	41	6	65
6	Rotherham	39	8	64
7	Exeter	39	12	63
8	Fleetwood	40	5	58
9	Southend	40	8	56
10	Oxford Utd	41	-6	56
11	**Bradford**	39	6	55
12	Chesterfield	39	7	53
13	Morecambe	41	-3	52
14	Bristol Rovers	39	-8	51
15	Wycombe	39	-10	49
16	Dag & Red	41	-3	48
17	Rochdale	40	-6	48
18	Wimbledon	41	-21	48
19	Torquay	41	-7	46
20	Accrington	41	-17	46
21	Barnet	41	-9	45
22	Plymouth	39	-8	43
23	Aldershot	40	-15	41
24	York	40	-16	41

Finishing Strong

"Another incredible chapter in a barely believable season was about to be written.."

One thing was certain. There was no room for manoeuvre. And when City went 1-0 down to a Joss Labadie strike after three minutes of the game at Torquay on Easter Monday, it really was looking bleak.

The renaissance began four minutes later, when Rory McArdle headed in a Gary Jones free-kick from eight yards.

And the Bantams were in front after 18 minutes via Garry Thompson's sizzler from the edge of the box, after Nahki Wells had challenged keeper Michael Poke for a ball that rebounded sideways.

City secured the points a couple of minutes after the break, when Thompson crossed deep for James Hanson to nod home at the far post.

Bradford were up to ninth and, with Exeter suffering a second successive Easter defeat, the gap between Phil Parkinson's side and the Grecians was just five points.

Game on.

Despite the win, City still required the sort of run their recent form suggested would be beyond them if they were going to get into the play-offs.

And they would need a favour or two from the sides above them, something Exeter appeared only too willing to provide.

Another of the teams battling for promotion, Northampton, were next up at Valley Parade and it was certain to be a bruising encounter against a team for whom the word 'battling' was surely coined.

The Cobblers are a typical Aidie Boothroyd outfit.

Robust and direct, when on-song, they pose a threat to anyone at League Two level.

They did cause a murmur or two by starting the game without either Ade Akinfenwa or Clive Platt, reducing the targets long-throw man Lee Tozer had to aim at.

Ironically it was a long ball from Garry Thompson that led to the only goal of the game.

Keeper Lee Nicholls and centre-back Nathan Cameron failed to deal with it and Nahki Wells chased down before turning it in from a yard out.

The win was a real boost and results elsewhere added to the jubilation felt around Valley Parade.

Fleetwood, Rotherham, Cheltenham and, most importantly, Exeter all lost.

On the back of two successive victories, City were now remarkably just two points outside the top seven with a game in hand. And it was Bristol Rovers next, when a win would take them above the dotted line for the first time since New Year's Day.

Rovers had started 2013 at the foot of the League Two table.

They arrived at Valley Parade on Tuesday 9 April 11th in the table and still with the faintest of outside hopes of a play-off place.

They were a far better side than the one that had shared six goals with City in November and there were some nerves among those gathering in the hours before kick-off.

Much of their post-Christmas success had been based on their decent home form, however.

And City, knowing victory would propel them into the play-off places, were soon in and among them.

Nahki Wells took just six minutes to head the Bantams in front. And he doubled their lead midway through the first half, when he scored from the spot after Ricky Ravenhill had been brought down by the magnificently-named Fabian Broghammer.

Andrew Davies' goal on the stroke of half-time settled any lingering nerves and the second half was a fairly routine affair. Tom Hitchcock pulled one back for Rovers before Garry Thompson continued his fine scoring form with City's fourth.

City had gone from ten points adrift just a few short weeks earlier to being a point in front of Exeter - and still with a game in hand.

Having been the hunter, City would find themselves the hunted in their next game. It was at Chesterfield who, like Bradford, had four games to play but were four points behind.

The stakes were high for both sides.

A City win would all but end the home side's hopes; a Chesterfield victory would keep them firmly in the hunt to take Bradford's place.

Over 7,000 crammed into the Proact Stadium to see the game and it did not disappoint.

Nahki Wells fired City ahead nine minutes before the break, only for Tendayi Darikwa to level with 20 minutes remaining.

It looked for all money as though Ricky Ravenhill's first goal of the campaign - a 79th-minute drive into the roof of the net - had given City the points, until Sam Togwell bagged a dramatic last-gasp leveller.

'It was really frustrating to concede like that, but we are pleased to be in there and we would certainly have taken this position a few weeks ago,' said Phil Parkinson, after watching his side fail in their bid for a fourth successive league win.

'It is a strong position to be in and we have two great games now at home to look forward to.'

There were three games in all - home to Rotherham and Burton, then away to Cheltenham. And it meant the Bantams were going to play three of the four sides immediately above them in the League Two standings.

First up were the Millers and that heralded the return to Valley Parade of Steve Evans who the previous season had been in charge of Crawley when City had three players red carded and Crawley two, with a third also dismissed retrospectively.

The Football Association took a dim view of an incident broadcast across the world and City were fined £9,000, with Crawley penalised to the tune of £18,000.

Andrew Davies and Claude Davis, involved in the end-of-game spat, were back in opposition again and more than an hour-and-a-half before kick-off Evans was shown his route to the dug-outs by a couple of burly stewards.

Just in case there was not enough tension, Evans had also had plenty to say about the respective merits of Valley Parade and his own club's New York Stadium.

City twice had the ball in the net in a goalless first half; James Hanson had a header ruled out for a push on Davis and the flag was up when Garry Thompson struck.

Bradford also had assistant manager Steve Parkin sent to the stands before the break and he could only watch as Rotherham struck twice in the last ten minutes.

Lee Frecklington scored from the penalty spot after a poor decision to penalise Michael Nelson for hand ball and, in the dying seconds, with Jon McLaughlin up for a corner, Kieran Agard broke clear to fire into an empty net.

McLaughlin did, at least, have the good sense not to haul the Rotherham man to the floor, something that would have resulted in a red card and a ban.

The win moved Rotherham into the top three - at the expense of City's next opponents Burton Albion - while the Bantams remained in the top seven, but with no real room for error.

And they went into the Saturday 20 April game with the Brewers knowing that, if they won and Exeter failed to pick up three points, they would achieve their play-off goal with a game to spare.

Burton arrived at Valley Parade on the back of successive home wins against Wycombe and Plymouth.

But their previous away game had resulted in a 7-1 thrashing at soon-to-be-promoted Port Vale.

They also knew that a victory would maintain their realistic hopes of going up automatically.

The game hinged on a couple of incidents in the couple of minutes before half-time, although Albion had surprised a few by playing just one striker in a game they really had to win.

James Hanson scored what turned out to be the only goal of the game after 44 minutes, when he looped the ball

You beauty: Alan Connell in celebratory mood *Gintare Karpaviciute*

into the net after Burton defender Marcus Holness failed to clear his lines.

And the visitors were reduced to ten men when skipper Lee Bell - he of the #whatcomesaroundgoesaround tweet back in October - was red-carded for a foul on Zavon Hines.

Perhaps unsurprisingly, Ricky Ravenhill, who had been sent off at Burton for his challenge on Bell, escorted the Albion man from the field with a smile on his face.

The only downside to the first half from a City point of view was an injury to winger Kyel Reid.

But Burton failed to make any real impression before or after the departures of Reid and Bell as City claimed the points.

Eyes had been as much on the vidiprinter as the Valley Parade pitch, with everyone eager for news from Exeter's home game with Cheltenham.

And the visitors were in front as early as the fifth minute thanks to a goal from Russell Penn.

That was also a one-goal game and the combination of results meant that - amazingly - City had clinched their top-seven place after 45 of the 46 scheduled league games.

It was Exeter's fifth defeat in six matches and they had picked up just one point from the 18 on offer, handing the initiative in no small part to City.

And the Bantams could travel to Cheltenham on the final day knowing that preparations for the play-offs had already begun. As a consequence, Phil Parkinson made eight changes to his side.

But, despite facing a full-strength Cheltenham who knew they had to win to maintain their hopes of an automatic place, City were able to come home with a point from a goalless draw.

That, and Burton's 3-2 win over champions Gillingham, meant the Bantams would face the Brewers over two legs for a place in the Wembley final, with Cheltenham taking on Northampton.

Another incredible chapter in a barely believable season was about to be written.

League Two

April 1 - Torquay United (A) W 3-1
City scorers: McArdle 7; Thompson 18; Hanson 47
McLaughlin, Darby, Meredith, McArdle, Davies, Jones, Ravenhill, Reid, Thompson, Hanson, Wells (Atkinson 85). Unused substitutes: Duke, McHugh, Connell, Hines, Nelson, Doyle.
Referee: Lewis. Attendance: 2,569

League Two

April 6 - Northampton Town (H) W 1-0
City scorer: Wells 24
McLaughlin, Darby, Davies, McArdle, Meredith, Thompson (Hines 72), Ravenhill, Jones, Reid, Hanson, Wells (Atkinson 90). Unused substitutes: Duke, McHugh, Connell, Nelson, Doyle.
Referee: Kettle. Attendance: 10,389

League Two

April 9 - Bristol Rovers (H) W 4-1
City scorers: Wells 6, 22 (pen); Davies 45, Thompson 58
McLaughlin, Darby, Davies, McArdle, Meredith, Thompson (Atkinson 77), Ravenhill, Jones (Doyle 72), Reid, Hanson, Wells (Connell 81). Unused substitutes: Duke, Hines, Nelson, McHugh,
Referee: Harrington. Attendance: 10,621

League Two
April 13 - Chesterfield (A) D 2-2
City scorers: Wells 36; Ravenhill 79
McLaughlin, Darby, Meredith, McArdle, Nelson, Jones, Ravenhill, Reid (Atkinson 46), Thompson (Hines 74), Hanson, Wells. Unused substitutes: Duke, McHugh, Connell, Doyle, Gray.
Referee: Malone. Attendance: 7,920

League Two
April 16 - Rotherham United (H) L 0-2
McLaughlin, Darby (Connell 81), McArdle, Davies (Nelson 25), Meredith (McHugh 50), Thompson, Ravenhill, Doyle, Reid, Hanson, Wells. Unused substitutes: Duke, Atkinson, Hines, Doyle.
Referee: Haywood. Attendance: 13,467

League Two
April 20 - Burton (H) W 1-0
City scorer: Hanson 44
McLaughlin, Darby, McArdle, Nelson, Meredith, Thompson (Atkinson 78), Ravenhill, Jones, Reid (Hines 19), Hanson, Wells (Connell 68). Unused substitutes: Duke, Gray, McHugh, Doyle.
Referee: Woolmer. Attendance: 13,235

League Two
April 27 - Cheltenham (A) D 0-0
Duke, Darby, Davies, Nelson, McHugh, Hines, Doyle, Ravenhill, Atkinson, Gray (Thompson 78), Connell (McArdle 62). Unused substitutes: McLaughlin, Meredith, Hanson, Jones, Wells.
Referee: D'Urso. Attendance: 5,888

League Two

Final table

		P	GD	Pts
1	Gillingham	46	27	83
2	Rotherham	46	15	79
3	Port Vale	46	35	78
4	Burton Albion	46	6	76
5	Cheltenham	46	7	75
6	Northampton	46	9	73
7	**Bradford**	46	11	69
8	Chesterfield	46	15	67
9	Oxford Utd	46	-1	65
10	Exeter	46	1	64
11	Southend	46	6	61
12	Rochdale	46	-2	61
13	Fleetwood	46	-2	60
14	Bristol Rovers	46	-9	60
15	Wycombe	46	-10	60
16	Morecambe	46	-6	58
17	York	46	-10	55
18	Accrington	46	-17	54
19	Torquay	46	-7	53
20	Wimbledon	46	-22	53
21	Plymouth	46	-9	52
22	Dag & Red	46	-7	51
23	Barnet	46	-12	51
24	Aldershot	46	-18	48

Gone for a Burton

"All was not lost, but the majority of the 14,657 knew that it would take another mammoth effort.."

Burton ended the regular season with the best home record in League Two - 17 wins from 23 games at the Pirelli Stadium.

In contrast, their form on their travels was patchy - just 22 points and five wins - so City knew they could steal a march on the opposition in the first leg in West Yorkshire.

There was a buoyant atmosphere around Valley Parade on Thursday 2 May. Everyone was confident that the Bantams would be able to build a sufficiently-impressive advantage to take to the Pirelli Stadium for the second leg.

So to say it was disappointing that City produced their worst defensive display of the entire campaign in the opening 45 minutes would be an understatement.

The early signs were not particularly bad, although why fourth-placed Burton were classed as underdogs was anyone's guess.

It started to unravel for City as their normally-reliable defence got the jitters. Calvin Zola capitalised, heading home the tie's opener before, from an offside position, doubling the lead six minutes later.

The Bantams' hopes appeared to be in tatters.

It took a fine save from Jon McLaughlin to keep it to two before the arrival of the lifeline Phil Parkinson's side required. Nahki Wells scored from the penalty spot after Damian McCrory handled in the area on the 39th minute.

There was still time for Robbie Weir to restore Albion's two-goal advantage before the break, but everyone inside Valley Parade knew City could not be as poor in the second half and the Bantams refused to lie down.

And sure enough there was an improvement, but the nerves were jangling until the 74th minute, when Garry Thompson picked the ball up on the right, cut inside and unleashed an unstoppable effort into the back of the net.

Parkinson looked an angry man when reflecting on the 3-2 loss - and rightly so.

'After the way we played in the first half I'm glad we're only one goal behind,' he told the assembled media.

'The play-offs can do strange things and we got punished. It was one of our poorest displays defensively, we didn't work as a unit.

'This group of players has been tremendous and we need another great performance on Sunday.'

All was not lost, but the majority of the 14,657 crowd knew that it would take another mammoth effort - in the 63rd game of the season at that - to book a second Wembley appearance in three months.

And only a fraction of those at the first leg would be able to get tickets for the second - a high noon showdown in the cramped surroundings of Burton's compact home.

But the 1,700 travelling supporters inside the Pirelli three days later were in fine voice more than an hour before kick-off, still believing there was one final twist to an already extraordinary season.

Burton began brightly but the game - and the tie as a whole - swung City's way on 27 minutes, after an error at the back from Marcus Holness.

He failed to deal with a long ball over the top and Nahki Wells nipped in to fire past the advancing Stuart Tomlinson.

It sent the fans into raptures and City were ahead in the tie for the first time five minutes after the break, when Wells' persistence created an opening for James Hanson, who drilled his right-footed shot beyond the reach of the keeper.

The visitors' joy, though, was short-lived as Burton made it 4-4 on aggregate from the penalty spot five minutes later. Jacques Maghoma scored after he had been brought down by an injudicious challenge from first-leg goal hero Garry Thompson.

Yet City were soon in front again - in a season like this, perhaps we shouldn't have been surprised - Wells claiming his second of the game and third of the tie from a Hanson knockdown.

Hanson then made a crucial block at the other end just before the final whistle, to ensure there would be no need for more energy-sapping extra-time.

And when the final whistle blew - in the seventh added minute - it sparked amazing scenes on and off the pitch, as City's players, fans and club staff celebrated the extension of the season by a further 13 days.

Wells and Hanson had been simply stunning in the second leg 3-1 victory and Phil Parkinson was quick to praise his strikeforce.

'The front two were unplayable today,' he said. 'We thought we'd change one or two things slightly to put them right up the pitch and it nullified them.

'Nahki's second was a real goalscorer's effort and Hanson's strike was a Premier League finish. His overall play is getting better and better.'

Only the most committed had given City a chance after their first-leg defeat.

But now they were returning to Wembley for a play-off final for the first time since 1996.

'You can't take away the enormity of the achievement,' Parkinson continued. 'When it mattered the most we produced and I think that's really important. Today was a massive test and we passed it.

'A lesser group of players wouldn't have responded in the way we did on Thursday.

'We said to the lads that if we could play in a disciplined, structured way then we'd have a great chance.'

A couple of players were unable to contain themselves, Carl McHugh and Andrew Davies both letting slip the f-word in live post-match interviews.

Skipper Gary Jones - the heartbeat of the side - also gave his reaction moments after the final whistle.

'We needed to come out all guns blazing today, because they did a number on us on Thursday,' he said.

'We were in a decent position because we knew what we needed to do - we had to win.

'When you've got Nahki Wells and James Hanson in your team you've got a chance. It was a great finish by James on his weaker foot.

'It'll be third time lucky for me at Wembley. I've lost there twice and now I want to lift some silverware.'

If anyone deserved to be a Wembley winner it was

Jones after the way he had led the side throughout the season. But he would have almost a fortnight to wait before he would be able to realise his dreams.

League Two Play-offs - Semi-final - First Leg
May 2 - Burton Albion (H) L 2-3
City scorers: Wells 38 (pen); Thompson 74
McLaughlin, Darby, Nelson, McArdle, Meredith, Thompson, Ravenhill (Doyle 57), Jones, Atkinson (Reid 57), Wells (Connell 89), Hanson. Unused substitutes: Duke, Gray, McHugh, Hines.
Referee: Adcock. Attendance: 14,657

League Two Play-offs - Semi-final - Second Leg
May 5 - Burton Albion (A) W 3-1 (*won 5-4 on agg*)
City scorers: Wells 27, 57; Hanson 50
McLaughlin, Darby, Meredith, Davies, McArdle, Reid (Atkinson 73), Thompson, Jones, Doyle, Hanson, Wells.
Unused substitutes: Duke, McHugh, Nelson, Ravenhill, Connell, Hines
Referee: Scott. Attendance: 6,148

Head and shoulders: Stephen Darby held aloft byHanson and Connell Gintare Karpaviciute

Wembley: Part Two.

"The play-off final was the culmination of a hard slog. And this match meant everything to everyone..."

The build-up to the play off final against Northampton Town was completely different to the Capital One Cup countdown.

There was far less national media interest in the game, although City taking part meant there was more than there might otherwise have been.

Manager Phil Parkinson strove to keep things as 'normal' as possible as his players prepared for 90 minutes that would decide whether or not they achieved the goal set for them almost ten months earlier.

The media day was on its usual Thursday, at the training ground rather than Valley Parade.

The only change was Friday's training venue, the players getting a run out at the Football Association's St George's Park facility, as they had done in the lead-up to the Aston Villa second leg League Cup clash.

This time it had nothing to do with the weather, though.

Parkinson knew that St George's Park had a pitch the same size as Wembley's and that ought to be perfect for his players to fine tune their games.

The manager also had time to reflect on how far the club had come in 12 months, having been looking over their shoulders at the League Two trapdoor in April 2012.

'Last year was really tough because there was so much hanging on us staying in the league,' he said.

'We set out a plan in the summer to move forward and I'd like to think, come Saturday evening, that can be completed. We know we've got to finish the job.

'We decided that we wanted to run with a smaller squad, but with better quality players.

'I felt last year that through the sheer number of players at the club there wasn't the spirit required to get the club to where it needs to be.

'We drew up a shortlist of players that we wanted based on character, athleticism and how close they lived to the ground, because I think that's important.

'We met with lots of players over the summer and some of them were bigger names than the ones we brought in, but I didn't feel they wanted to be here for the right reason.

'Our aim was to put together a group of players that, if we progress as a club, and hopefully we will this season, they can play in a higher division.

'The last thing you want is to get promoted and have to make wholesale changes.'

Parkinson had promotion on his mind, but Northampton would be a robust obstacle in their way.

As in the build-up, the day of the play-off final - Saturday 18 May - could hardly have been more different to the lead-up to the Capital One Cup clash with Swansea.

Many of the City fans who had made a weekend of it in February decided that it was a there-and-back trip for the Northampton game.

And despite the kick-off being a full two-and-a-half hours earlier, Wembley Way was strangely quiet in the morning.

Where Bradford and Swansea fans had revelled in their teams' achievements in getting to a major cup final, there were far fewer from either West Yorkshire or Northamptonshire in late April.

And those who were there were very nervous.

The Swansea game had been a bonus for both sides it seemed; and both sets of fans were determined to enjoy it.

The play-off was the culmination of a hard slog from late summer, through autumn and winter and into the spring.

And this match meant everything to everyone.

The City players were in business-as-usual mode as they made their way to the national stadium.

When they arrived at Wembley they were in tracksuits rather than cup final suits, and it was straight onto the pitch for a quick read of the programme and the usual pre-match banter between teammates.

Everything had been kept as normal as it could have been, given the magnificent surroundings.

In contrast, Northampton were 'suited and booted' and several of their players gazed open-mouthed at the stadium when they walked out onto the turf - many for the first time.

City had, or so it felt at the time, won the first round.

Now they just had to finish the job - and the final could hardly have started any better.

Northampton boss Aidie Boothroyd, Bradford born and bred, had tried to suggest City's players would be scarred by their experience against Swansea.

He clearly felt that no side could recover from the public mauling Phil Parkinson's team had suffered at the hands of the Premier League stars.

But Boothroyd had not seen the reaction of the City players in the wake of their heavy defeat.

They near-enough acknowledged that it had been a game too far for them and they knew that there had been nothing more they could have done.

Their previous Wembley experience certainly appeared to be helping the Bantams in the early stages, with Northampton playing like a side who were startled by their surroundings.

And City were already well on top by the time they took a 15th-minute lead, James Hanson - in his 59th game of the campaign - looping a header home from Garry Thompson's cross.

Three minutes later it was 2-0, as Rory McArdle stole in at the near post to get on the end of Nathan Doyle's ball in and his bullet header crashed into the net.

City's fans were in dreamland.

And it was all over before the game had even reached the half-hour when Thompson nodded a Kyel Reid cross back from the right hand side of the six yard box for Nahki Wells, who stretched out a leg to volley home.

There were other chances - Reid had a close-range header tipped over the bar, Wells was denied by the keeper and Thompson pulled one wide.

But it is doubtful whether many of the Bradford fans

saw them, and fewer cared because they were already in celebration mode.

Nor did it matter that City were unable to add to their goal tally because Northampton posed little or no threat in the hour of the game that remained.

Unlike the aftermath of the Capital One Cup final, half the stadium was empty when team skipper Gary Jones and Ricky Ravenhill, the man from whom he had taken the armband, lifted the play-off final winners' trophy.

But City were happy to celebrate their triumph at their fans' end of the ground and they had every right to do so. It had been the perfect plan, perfectly executed.

'I was really pleased and couldn't have asked any more from the lads,' said 'Parkinson in the tunnel after the game. 'To be 3-0 up at half-time was a dream really.

'It was important [at the break] that we didn't get carried away and I have said many times this season that this team is going to run, chase and tackle to the last minute of the last game.

'I said to them we weren't there yet - we had another 49 minutes to go, so we had to make sure we finished it off and did the job. The professionalism and ruthlessness about the way we played in the second half pleased me as much as the first half.'

The City boss added that it had been a deliberate ploy to try to make the final just like any other away game.

'We kept everything on the periphery away this time and focused on what we had to do,' he said.

'I think the experience of coming here before certainly helped us, because it can be draining.'

While Parkinson's side had held no surprises to the seasoned City watcher, the Northampton starting XI did, with Ade Akinfenwa only named among the substitutes.

'I can't lie, I was pleased,' said Parkinson, when quizzed about the big striker's absence from the starting line-up.

'I was pleased because he is a player who can produce on the big day - we have seen it before.

'He is their top scorer, even though he hasn't scored for a long time, so it was a bonus when we got their team.

'Without meaning to be conceited, I looked at it (their team) and thought we have got a great chance.

'They came with quite an open side and when teams have done that against us this season we have, more or less, punished them.'

Ultimately, the key to the victory had been City's positive approach and the two goals in quick succession scored by Hanson and McArdle.

'I have said all season that when we are at our best we have the power and pace, but we also have the ability to play and it kind of worked perfectly,' said Parkinson.

'The size of the pitch suited the running ability of Hanson and Wells and the slickness suited Jones and Doyle in the middle.

'I thought we got the balance just right.

'It was strange in the second half with seven minutes to go. They [the fans] didn't want to celebrate, because we weren't there yet.

'Then, with 84 or 85 minutes on the clock, I could sense the belief in the ground.

'I tried my best not to look at the clock, then Steve [Parkin] told me how much time was going to be added on.

'With four minutes to go and three goals there would have had to have been a travesty to lose.'

McArdle also pointed to the swift start as one of the key components of the Bradford success.

'We knew that if we set out as we have done in the past month or so we would give ourselves a chance of winning the game,' he said.

'And we could not have asked for more than the start we had.

'I thought we were cruising and they didn't cause us too many problems.

'We worked on a high tempo start in training and the game plan ticked all the boxes.

'We were expecting Northampton to make a charge at the start of the second half and they did in spells, but I don't think Jon [McLaughlin] really had a save to make in 90 minutes.

'The timings of the goals were perfect and really took the sting out of Northampton.

'The first one was good, then we got the second soon after and a third knocked the stuffing out of them.'

McArdle added that City just had to keep going after the break to ensure there was no chance of a Northampton fightback.

'It was important that we carried on doing in the second half what we had done in the first,' he said.

'We had to make sure that we didn't get complacent and start trying to do things we don't normally do.

'All credit to the Gaffer and Steve Parkin for making sure no one lost focus.'

Given that it was Bradford's 64th game of the campaign, they might have been forgiven for flagging as the game wore on.

But there was no sign of that, a fact that was clearly down to the club's fitness regime.

'Credit has to go to Nick Allamby for that,' said McArdle. 'It was the first time I had worked with him when

I came in for pre-season and I have nothing but the highest regard for him.

'It is not just the science side that he brings to it, but his personality and how he interacts with the lads.

'Everyone has respect for him.

'It was our 64th game, but looking at the way we were it could easily have been our first.'

The fact that City had been so relaxed in the build-up might have surprised a few people.

And the fact that the approach was so familiar to the players had clearly helped.

'The spirit was good on the way to the match - the music was on and it was just any other game,' said McArdle.

'We rolled up in tracksuits, which some people might have found surprising.

'I think that showed in how relaxed everyone was and how we took to the occasion.'

The Wembley win capped a magnificent season for everyone connected with the club.

And it came just a few days after the presentation evening at which full-back Stephen Darby had received the players' player of the year trophy.

'It has been unbelievable,' said the former Liverpool youngster.

'The run we went on to get to the League Cup final and then to come back to the play-offs and win, it has been magnificent. I am just delighted for everyone involved with the football club.

'From the first game of the season the fans have been unbelievable. They stuck by us and believed in us.'

Darby added that the game against Swansea a couple of months earlier had been a key factor in City's success.

'We knew it was going to be a different game,' he said.

'Being here before probably helped and I think it showed with a tremendous performance.

'We could not have got off to a better start and we managed to see it out.'

When City set out at the start of the season in August, no one could have predicted how things would turn out.

The club had pushed the boat out to a degree in assembling a high quality squad of players.

And there was no doubt in anyone's minds what the target for 2012-13 had been - promotion.

'It was our aim at the start of the season - everyone knew that,' said play-off final goalscorer McArdle.

'To get to the League Cup final was massive, but in hindsight we probably did lose a little track on the league.

'We knew that was the main focus and in the last two months of the campaign we gave it a real charge.

'Here we are now having achieved everything we set out to do and possibly a little bit more.'

McArdle's admission that the team's league form had suffered in the wake of the Capital One cup final came as no surprise.

Nor did the dip in form itself, something manager Phil Parkinson knew might happen.

'I have played in teams that have won titles and managed teams that have got promotion,' he said.

'And even in those teams you get ups and downs.

'When the road becomes a bit bumpy, that is when you have to stick together and we have done that all season.

'We never lost the belief that we could do it and we have got over the finishing line.

'I am just so pleased that when it mattered most the lads have delivered a really good performance.'

League Two Play-offs - Final
May 18 - Northampton Town (Wembley) W 3-0
Hanson 15 McArdle 19 Wells 28
McLaughlin, Darby, McArdle, Davies, Meredith, Thompson, Doyle (Ravenhill 87), Jones, Reid (Atkinson 78), Wells (Connell 84), Hanson. Substitutes not used: Nelson, Hines, McHugh, Duke.
Referee: Stroud. Attendance: 47,127

A Season to Remember.

Who knew that a late-summer trip to the East Midlands would end up being the start of a journey into history?

No one could have - but for Bradford City an extra-time win over Notts County on August 11 proved to be just that.

My decision to take on the job of the BBC's man covering Bradford City was met with little more than a ripple of excitement among my closest friends and ex-colleagues.

Having spent the previous eight years watching, in a professional capacity, varying levels of non-league football at places like Clitheroe and Retford, I must say the 'bright lights' of Valley Parade held a certain appeal.

True, City had spent a couple of seasons languishing in the wrong half of the bottom tier of the Football League.

But no one should ever forget the heady days of the Premier League; the drama of their last-day survival in 2000;

Reach out and touch: A City fan gets closer to the League Two trophy Gintare Karpaviciute

the potential of a club that had won the FA Cup a mere 101 years previously.

That might be stretching it a touch.

But there is little doubt that if the tag 'sleeping giant' should be applied to any football club, Bradford City and its magnificent fan base are it.

Dave Fletcher, June 2013

Afterword.

By Gary Jones

For the six years they had been in League Two the Bradford fans had had nothing but doom and gloom.

And to come out and support the team like they did is quite remarkable.

The average crowd of 10,000 is quite ridiculous for a League Two side - they are unbelievable.

I was just glad that we were able to give them a team they could be proud of and relate to.

Relating to your team is very important and they have seen the hard work and graft the lads put in.

When you leave a club after a long time you always dream something good will happen.

And I think 2012-13 was my best as a professional.

As you get older you have to look after yourself even more, and fitness coach Nick Allamby knows when to train me and when to give me a rest.

That proved vital last season and hopefully it will be the same this coming season too. A lot of teams that go up from League Two do quite well in League One.

It is all down to momentum and here at Bradford City we have the nucleus of a good squad.

Players will come and players will go, it is important we get the right characters to come into the squad.

At Valley Parade, we work 100 per cent for each other and long may that be so.

npower
npower
BC
AFC
THE BANTAMS
NORTHAMPTON TOWN F.C.

THE STORY OF FOOTBALL:

via the Moors, Dales and Wolds of England's largest and proudest county

YORKSHIRE FOOTBALL - A HISTORY

Cameron Fleming

ISBN: 978-0956252654

Scratching Shed Publishing Ltd